DOMINOES

The Secret Agent

Joseph Conrad

Founder Editors: Bill Bowler and Sue Parminter

Text adaptation by Lesley Thompson

Illustrated by Mike Redman and Carlo Molinari

Joseph Conrad (1857–1924) was born in Poland. By the age of eleven, both his parents had died, and in 1874 Conrad moved to France, and later to England, and began working as a sailor. He spent nearly twenty years at sea on voyages that took him to many corners of the world, giving him ideas for many of his novels like *Typhoon*, which is also available as a Domino. He chose to write in English and his first novel, *Almayer's Folly*, was published in 1894. The same year, at the age of thirty-seven, Conrad married an English woman sixteen years younger than himself. *The Secret Agent* was published in 1907.

Great Clarendon Street, Oxford, OX2 6DP,
United Kingdom

Oxford University Press is a department of the University of Oxford.
It furthers the University's objective of excellence in research, scholarship,
and education by publishing worldwide. Oxford is a registered trade
mark of Oxford University Press in the UK and in certain other countries

First published in Dominoes 2020
2024 2023 2022 2021 2020
10 9 8 7 6 5 4 3 2 1

ISBN: 978 0 19 460830 5 Book
ISBN: 978 0 19 460829 9 Book and Audio Pack

Audio not available separately

Printed in China

This book is printed on paper from certified and
well-managed sources.

ACKNOWLEDGEMENTS

Story illustrations and cover artwork by: Mike Redman/Advocate Art and Carlo Molinari/Advocate Art.

Additional illustrations by: Gavin Reece p.75.

The publisher would like to thank the following for permission to reproduce photographs: Bridgeman Art Library Ltd p.70 (Port Light, Grimshaw, John Atkinson (1836–93)/Private Collection/© Mallett Gallery, London, UK); Getty Images pp.27 (Greenwich Observatory/Richard T. Nowitz), 76 (Charles Genevieve Louis Auguste Timothee D'Eon De Beaumont/Bettmann), 76 (Guy Burgess/Bettmann); Mary Evans Picture Library p (Greenwich Observatory postcard/P S & V (Lewisham)); Rex Shutterstock p.74 (Mata Hari/Gianni Dagli Orti).

Contents

ACTIVITIES

BEFORE READING

1 ***The Secret Agent* is about a terrorist attack in London in 1886. Here are some people from the story.**

What do you think happens in the story? Look at the pictures and answer these questions. Use a dictionary to help you.

a Who is the secret agent?

b Who dies in an explosion?

c Who is murdered?

d Who kills themselves?

2 This building is the Royal Observatory at Greenwich. What is it?

a ☐ the most important police office in England

b ☐ a place where you can study the stars

c ☐ the place where the King of England lives in London

A visit to the embassy

Mr Verloc went out that morning leaving his young **brother-in-law** taking care of the shop and his wife taking care of his brother-in-law. The shop was a small dark building, which stood in a narrow street in Soho, London. In the window there were photographs of dancing girls wearing very few clothes and beside these there were mysterious packets, yellow **envelopes**, bottles of **ink**, old books and newspapers. There were two **gas** lights in the window, but these never burned strongly at night, perhaps in order to save money, or perhaps to make it difficult to see customers going into the shop.

The door was closed during the day. In the evening it was left half open. Few people came into the shop. They were usually men in cheap clothes who entered in a secretive way with their faces half hidden by their hats and coats. Each time a customer arrived, an old **cracked** bell rang to warn the people in the house behind the shop.

Mr Verloc owned the shop and the house. At the sound of the bell, he usually came out of the room behind the shop. He was a large man with a dangerous look hidden in his sleepy eyes. While he stared at them, customers gave him money and he gave them what they asked for. Everything was strangely expensive in that dark little shop of his.

Sometimes, Mrs Verloc appeared. She was young with a full figure, clear skin, and tidy hair. The younger men felt uncomfortable with her. If she came out to help them, they usually bought something that they did not really want, like a bottle of ink, and then dropped it on the ground outside the shop when they left. The men who came in the evening were different. They spoke to Mrs Verloc in a friendly way as they went through the shop into the back room. The shop door was the only entrance to the house.

brother-in-law your wife's or husband's brother

envelope a paper cover that you put a letter in

ink you put this in a pen in order to write with it; the words on this page are made with black ink

gas something that gives light or heat in lamps or cookers

cracked broken by a thin line

Mr Verloc lived in the house with his wife, Winnie, her brother, Stevie, and her mother. Winnie's mother was a fat woman who could not walk very well. Her husband, who had owned a pub, was dead and for years she kept a house where gentlemen could **rent** rooms in Belgravia, a quiet part of London. Mr Verloc had sometimes taken rooms there. He travelled **abroad** on business, but nobody really knew what he did. When he was in London, he stayed in bed until very late. He went out in the evening and came back at three or four o'clock in the morning. Winnie took his breakfast to him in bed. She was pleasant, but she did not say much. Mr Verloc thought she was pretty, and he began to speak more often to her mother. Winnie's mother thought that Mr Verloc was a nice, **respectable** gentleman, but he did not take Winnie out at night to the theatre like nice respectable gentlemen usually do. He was busy in the evenings.

rent to give money every month for somewhere to live

abroad in or to another country

respectable that people think is good

After a short time, Mr Verloc and Winnie were married. He told her that his work was **political** and that she would have to be pleasant to his political friends. Winnie agreed to do what he asked and they moved to Soho.

'Of course we'll take care of your furniture, Mother,' Winnie had said.

Winnie's mother left Belgravia, and she and Stevie went to live in Soho, too. Now Mr Verloc had a respectable family. Winnie's mother felt safe with Mr Verloc. She thought that her daughter and son Stevie were safe, too.

Feeling safe was important, because Stevie was a problem. Although he was old enough to have a beard, which was starting to grow on his **weak** face, he was like a little child. When he had to take a message to someone, he often got lost. He forgot his address and when he was worried he **stuttered**. He got a job as an office-boy when he was fourteen, but one day he exploded some **fireworks** on the stairs and the other workers were frightened. Some of the other young office boys had given him the idea, and he was easily excited by things that he heard or saw. After that, Stevie lost his job, of course, and he had to wash plates and clean shoes at home instead. He had no future. Winnie's mother was very happy that Mr Verloc was so kind and wanted to take care of all her family.

In the house in Soho, Stevie tried to help his sister. He loved her and was happy to do anything for her. In his free time, he sat in the kitchen and spent hours drawing circles on pieces of paper. Winnie watched him carefully. She was like a mother to him.

This then was the house and family that Mr Verloc left behind him as he walked west through London at 10.30 in the morning. He was going to a foreign **embassy** in Knightsbridge, a rich part of London. It was his second visit in eleven years. He wore a dark coat and a hat, his boots shone, and his hair was carefully brushed.

The sun was red over London that morning and there was a

political to do with people who decide what should happen in a country

weak not strong

stutter to have difficulty speaking and to repeat the start of words

firework something that burns with coloured lights and a loud noise

embassy the office of people working for their country abroad

protect to take care of

porter a person at the entrance to a building who meets visitors

golden light in the air. The roofs of the buildings were red-gold in the sun and the back of Verloc's coat was touched with red too, like old gold. But Verloc did not feel old.

As he walked past Hyde Park, he noticed rich people riding their horses and walking in the park, and thought: 'We must **protect** the money at the heart of this city, at the heart of this country, from the poor.' But his face did not show his feelings. Showing feelings was hard work and Verloc was lazy.

He turned left into a quieter, smaller street. All the windows in the houses here were bright and clean and their front doors shone. Everything here seemed so empty and so strangely unreal, that it was like a dream which went on for ever.

At the entrance to the Embassy, Verloc showed the **porter** a special embassy envelope and continued on his way through the embassy garden. He showed the same envelope to another man who opened the front door of the embassy building. He was then taken through a large entrance hall and upstairs into a small

room with a writing table and two chairs in it. Here he waited, standing, with his hat and his stick in his hand. After some time, another door opened quietly and a man entered carrying some papers. He had an ugly, white face with long, thin, grey hairs on the top of his head. He put on some glasses and Verloc's appearance seemed at once to surprise him. This was Wurmt, the **Ambassador's assistant**. Neither he nor Verloc said hello.

'I have some of your reports here,' said Wurmt in a tired voice. 'We do not like the way the police act in this country.'

Verloc spoke for the first time that morning.

'Every country has its police. I can't do anything about that.'

'What we want,' replied Wurmt, 'is something to wake the police up. You can do that, can't you?'

Verloc said nothing, but he **sighed**. Then, realizing his mistake, he immediately tried to smile.

'The **law** is too soft here,' continued Wurmt, staring through his glasses at Verloc. 'And some people aren't very happy about that—'

'No, they aren't,' interrupted Verloc. 'My reports from the last twelve months say that clearly.'

'I have read your reports,' replied Wurmt softly. 'But I don't understand why you wrote them.'

There was silence. Verloc bit his lip and Wurmt looked down at the papers on the table in front of him. At last, he continued.

'Everything in these reports was already known when you began working for us. We want to hear something important, something surprising, something new.'

'I shall try in future to please you,' said Verloc uncomfortably.

Wurmt stared at Verloc.

'You are very **overweight**,' he said.

'Overweight?' said Verloc angrily. He could not believe what he was hearing.

Wurmt did not answer for some time. In the end, he said, 'I think you should see Mr Vladimir. Please wait here.'

ambassador an important person who speaks for their country abroad

assistant helper

sigh to blow out air from your mouth with a sad or tired sound

law something decided by the government that tells people what they must or must not do

overweight too heavy or fat

ACTIVITIES

READING CHECK

Choose the right words to finish the sentences.

a The story begins when Verloc …
- **1** ☑ goes out to visit the Embassy.
- **2** ☐ sells his shop to Stevie.
- **3** ☐ comes out to help a customer.

b Verloc is a …
- **1** ☐ man who believes that the poor should get rich people's money.
- **2** ☐ large man who has a dangerous look in his eyes.
- **3** ☐ hard-working man who never does anything wrong.

c Winnie's brother, Stevie, …
- **1** ☐ acts like a child.
- **2** ☐ has a strong face.
- **3** ☐ works as an office-boy.

d Winnie's mother …
- **1** ☐ knows all about Verloc's business.
- **2** ☐ lives in a house in Belgravia.
- **3** ☐ thinks that Winnie and Stevie are safe with Verloc.

e Winnie …
- **1** ☐ agrees to be pleasant to Verloc's friends.
- **2** ☐ enjoys going out to the theatre with Verloc.
- **3** ☐ likes talking about herself.

f Wurmt thinks that …
- **1** ☐ Verloc's reports are very useful.
- **2** ☐ Verloc is lazy.
- **3** ☐ the British police are too hard.

WORD WORK

1 Use these words to complete the sentences.

Ambassador	**embassy**	**envelopes**	**fireworks**
gas	**ink**	**law**	**political**
porter	~~**rented**~~	**respectable**	**stutters**

a Before he married, Verloc …rented… rooms from Winnie's mother.

b When he married, Verloc told Winnie that he did ……………… work.

c Verloc seems to be a very ……………… gentleman with a shop and a family.

d The story happens in 1886 so there are ……………… lights in Verloc's shop.

e Some of the things in the shop are sold in yellow ……………… .

f Young men buy a bottle of ……………… from Winnie Verloc instead of photographs of dancers.

g When he's excited or worried, Stevie ....

h Stevie lost an office job because he exploded .... on the stairs.

i That morning, Verloc goes to an .... building in Knightsbridge.

j Verloc has to show an important letter to the .... outside the building.

k Wurmt works for a very important man – the ....

l In Britain and other countries it is against the .... to make bombs.

2 Find words from Chapter 1 to match the underlined words in the sentences.

a Stevie is Verloc's wife's brother. ..brother-in-law..

b Before he married Verloc travelled to other countries a lot. ....

c Stevie, Winnie's younger brother, is not strong. ....

d Verloc wants to take care of the money at the heart of London. ....

e The bell in Verloc's shop is broken by a thin line. ....

f Wurmt is the Ambassador's helper. ....

g Verloc blows air out of his mouth noisily. ....

h Wurmt says that Verloc is fat. ....

GUESS WHAT

What do you think happens in the next chapter? Choose the words to complete the sentences.

a Verloc *enjoys* / *doesn't enjoy* his meeting with Mr Vladimir.

b Mr Vladimir tells Verloc to *work harder* / *sell the shop.*

c Verloc must *plant a bomb* / *kill a policeman.*

d Verloc *tells* / *doesn't tell* Winnie about his visit to the Embassy.

e Winnie gets worried about *Stevie* / *Verloc.*

f Stevie thinks Verloc's political friends are *funny* / *frightening.*

Back to the shop

VERLOC waited in the little room. After a short time, a servant appeared and took him upstairs to the first floor. There, Verloc entered a large room where a thin young man with a short beard sat at a big desk. The man spoke in French to Wurmt, who was leaving. 'You are quite right, my dear Wurmt. But he's not just overweight. He's fat – the animal.'

Mr Vladimir, the **First Secretary**, was always invited to parties. He was a good speaker and when he told his funny stories he had smiling eyes. But, when he looked at Verloc, his face was hard and cold.

'You understand French, I suppose?'

Verloc said that he did and added in a low voice that he had lived for some years in France.

Vladimir continued: 'How long were you in prison for stealing the plans for that new French gun?'

'Five years,' replied Verloc.

Vladimir laughed unpleasantly. 'That wasn't very good getting caught like that! What happened?'

'I fell in love with a woman and she wasn't honest with me. I was young,' added Verloc, feeling stupid.

'Ah, so she got the money and then sold you to the police.'

'Yes,' said Verloc, hating the conversation.

'How long have you worked for the Embassy here?'

'Eleven years. I began when Baron Stott-Wartenheim was Ambassador in Paris. He ordered me to come to London. I am English, but my father was French—'

Vladimir interrupted him. 'Well, times have changed since then. The secret service gave people money for nothing in those days. Look at you! One of the hungry workers! What are you anyway – an **anarchist**?'

First Secretary
a very important person working at an embassy

anarchist
a person who believes that laws are not necessary

'That's right,' said Verloc.

'Ridiculous! You are too fat for an anarchist. And I'll tell you why – you are lazy. What we want now is action, do you hear?'

Verloc was now both angry and worried. What did this man want from him?

'A secret agent has to do something,' went on Vladimir angrily. 'The good times are finished. You must work for your money now!'

'Don't speak to me like that!' Verloc felt hot and his clothes felt uncomfortable. Vladimir spoke again:

'There is a meeting in Milan soon on international crime, and we must do something before that to wake up the people here. England is too soft. Your anarchist friends do just what they like! They should all be in prison. The middle classes here **support** the people who want to rob them! Don't you agree?'

'Yes,' said Verloc, who was beginning to lose his voice.

'What they need is something to frighten them. It's time your friends acted.'

Verloc was silent. In his opinion, Vladimir knew nothing about the real methods of the **revolutionary** world.

'We want to change people's opinion and make them support harder laws. We want an attack on something that the middle classes think is important. **Science** for example. **Astronomy**.'

'Astronomy?' Verloc could not hide his surprise.

support to agree with and to help somebody or something

revolutionary wanting to change things quickly, and sometimes violently

science the study of the natural world

astronomy the study of the stars and planets

'Yes. I want you to put a bomb under **Greenwich Observatory**. You can use that old **terrorist**, Yundt. Or Michaelis, the man who was in prison. You'll get no more money until something happens. What is your job supposed to be anyway?'

'I have a shop. My wife helps me.'

'Your wife! Anarchists don't have wives!'

'That isn't any of your business!'

'Oh yes it is,' Vladimir said coldly. 'You have one month. If you don't **plant** the bomb by then, your job with us is finished.'

Vladimir got up from his seat and turned his back on Verloc. He watched in the mirror as the secret agent left the room.

Verloc left the Embassy in an angry dream and walked back to the shop. Afterwards, he could not remember anything about his journey home.

Winnie heard the sound of the cracked bell and looked into the shop. She saw her husband sitting in the dark room and returned to making the lunch. Verloc sat without moving, his hat pushed back on his head. An hour later, when his wife went to tell him that lunch was ready, he had not moved from his chair.

At lunch, Verloc was silent. Stevie was quiet and good, but the two women watched him closely because they did not want him to worry Verloc.

In the sitting room of Verloc's house, a small group of men sat and talked in front of the fire.

One of them was Michaelis, a fat, white-skinned man. He had spent fifteen years in prison and was now out **on bail**. He had an open, honest-looking face and smiled a lot.

Karl Yundt, who called himself the 'terrorist', was still wearing his coat and hat inside the warm room. Yundt frightened people with his violent opinions and he enjoyed doing it. At the moment, he was arguing for 'death used in the service of humanity'.

'But will that really help us?' asked Michaelis, standing up.

'You're so **pessimistic**,' Yundt said angrily.

Greenwich /ˈgrenɪtʃ/

observatory a building where scientists watch the stars

terrorist a person who tries to get political change by doing violent things with guns and bombs

plant to leave (a bomb) somewhere

on bail when a prisoner can leave prison before finishing his time there because he promises to do nothing wrong

pessimistic thinking that bad things will happen

'That's not true,' cried Michaelis. 'I'm not pessimistic, I'm **optimistic** – I believe that things will change, but there is no need for a revolution.'

There was another man in the room, sitting by the window. This was **Comrade** Ossipon. He was younger than the others, not bad-looking, with fair hair and a red face. Ossipon was an ex-medical student who wrote for a political group called the *Future of the* ***Proletariat***. Now he sat listening to the others with an amused look on his face.

The room was getting hot. Verloc got up slowly and opened the door into the kitchen. Stevie was sitting quietly at the kitchen table drawing circles as usual.

Ossipon walked into the kitchen and looked over Stevie's shoulder with scientific interest.

'Those drawings show us that the boy has a criminal mind,' he said.

optimistic thinking that good things will happen

comrade a person with the same political ideas, like a brother

proletariat working people

'Does he look like a criminal to you?' said Verloc looking interested for the first time in hours.

'Yes. Just look at his ears. Lombroso talks about ears like that in his book.'

'Lombroso is stupid,' said Karl Yundt, who was listening to the conversation. 'You can't recognize criminals by their teeth or ears. Criminals aren't born that way. Why don't you talk about the people who make them into criminals? What about the law that marks them, that burns their skin for life? Can't you see the red burns and smell the burning? Forget Lombroso and his stupid ideas!'

Stevie was now standing at the door. He heard Yundt's angry words and they frightened him. His mouth fell open.

Michaelis smiled. 'We must watch and wait calmly. Better times are coming for the poor people, you'll see.' Stevie calmed down a little at these words.

The discussion continued. Verloc said little and stared into space. Stevie sat in the doorway, frightened by the men's words. After a while, the men left the house and Verloc closed the door violently behind them. None of them could help him, that was sure. So who was going to plant Vladimir's bomb? Verloc could not do it himself. If he was not careful, his future as a secret agent could be in danger. Those men were so lazy, he thought. Yundt was looked after by a rich old woman and when she died, he thought, Yundt's love of revolution would probably die too. Michaelis was supported by another rich lady who let him stay at her house in the country. And Ossipon also lived well thanks to the young women who paid for everything that he needed.

It was different for himself, thought Verloc. He had to look after Winnie.

Before he went to bed, Verloc looked at the few coins that they had taken that day in the shop. 'How can we live without the money from the Embassy?' he thought.

Stevie was still in the kitchen, walking round and round the table with a worried look on his face. Verloc did not know what to say to him. It was strange: he lived with this young man and paid for all his needs, but he had no idea how to talk to him.

'Why don't you go to bed now?' he said after some time. Stevie did not answer. He left the boy in the kitchen and went upstairs. He could hear the old woman talking in her sleep through the wall of her bedroom. 'Another one to look after,' he thought angrily.

Winnie was asleep, but he woke her up and told her that Stevie was still downstairs. She said nothing, but got up immediately and left the room.

Verloc got ready for bed. He felt alone and sorry for himself. He seemed to see Vladimir's long, thin face laughing at him in the dark.

'I don't feel very well,' he told Winnie when she came back.

'That poor boy is very excited tonight,' she replied.

Verloc was not interested in talking about Stevie. Why didn't she talk about him and his feelings? Wasn't he her husband?

'I haven't been feeling well for the last few days,' he said. He wanted to tell Winnie about the Embassy, the bomb, everything. But Winnie still wanted to talk about Stevie.

'He hears too many things that he doesn't understand,' she said, thinking about the men who visited them in the evenings. She hated Karl Yundt with his talk of death and violence, but she did not mind Michaelis who was kinder. She said nothing about Ossipon because she did not want to think about him; he made her feel uncomfortable.

'Stevie's been reading those stupid *Future of the Proletariat* stories again,' she continued. 'He read about a soldier cutting off someone's ear and wanted to kill the soldier. I had to take the **carving knife** off him. Why do they write things like that?'

Verloc did not answer.

'Are you comfortable, Adolf, dear? Shall I put out the light now?'

'Yes. Put it out,' said Verloc. But he knew that he was not going to sleep well that night.

carving knife
a big knife for cutting meat

ACTIVITIES

READING CHECK

Are these sentences true or false? Tick the boxes.

		True	False
a	Mr Vladimir thinks that Verloc is a good secret agent.	☐	☑
b	Mr Vladimir laughs at Verloc because he was sent to prison.	☐	☐
c	Mr Vladimir tells Verloc that now he must work for the money that he gets from the Embassy.	☐	☐
d	Mr Vladimir tells Verloc that he must plant a bomb in Greenwich to frighten the middle classes.	☐	☐
e	Yundt tells the others that Stevie has a criminal way of thinking.	☐	☐
f	Lombroso wrote a book about how to recognize a criminal.	☐	☐
g	Verloc chooses one of his friends to help him with the Greenwich bomb.	☐	☐
h	Winnie and her family help Verloc to stop worrying about his problems.	☐	☐

WORD WORK

1 Match the words in the bomb with the correct definitions.

a First Secretary a very important person working at an embassy

b .... someone with the same political ideas

c .... someone who thinks there should be no laws

d .... someone who tries to get political change by doing violent things

e .... working people

2 Find words from Chapter 2 to complete the sentences.

a Mr Vladimir tells Verloc to p lant the bomb within a month or he will lose his job.

b Mr Vladimir says the English middle classes are stupid because they don't work against people who want to take rich people's money; they s _ _ _ _ _ _ them.

c Mr Vladimir wants to change the ideas of the middle classes by attacking s _ _ _ _ _ _.

d Mr Vladimir doesn't really know what the r _ _ _ _ _ _ _ _ _ _ _ _ _ world is like.

e The Greenwich O _ _ _ _ _ _ _ _ _ _ _ is famous, so a bomb exploding there will be in all the newspapers.

f Famous people, like Edmond Halley, have studied a _ _ _ _ _ _ _ _ _ at Greenwich.

g Michaelis is o _ _ _ _ _ _ _ _ _ _; he believes that things will get better.

h Michaelis is out of prison o _ b _ _ _ because he promises to do nothing wrong.

i The opposite of optimistic is p _ _ _ _ _ _ _ _ _ _ _; always seeing the bad side of everything.

j Winnie is worried about Stevie cutting himself when he plays with a c _ _ _ _ _ _ k _ _ _ _ after reading a violent political story.

GUESS WHAT

Match the first and second parts of these sentences to find out what happens in the next chapter.

a There is a story in the newspapers about ...

b Comrade Ossipon meets another anarchist to talk about ...

c No one knows ...

d Ossipon is worried about ...

e The anarchist tells Ossipon to go and speak to ...

1 the police.

2 Winnie Verloc.

3 the news of the Greenwich bomb.

4 where Verloc is.

5 a bomb in Greenwich Park.

A bomb in Greenwich Park

THE bar, which was below ground, had a low roof, no windows, and pictures of people drinking and dancing on the walls. At one of the thirty small tables sat Comrade Ossipon. Opposite him there was a dirty little man who was drinking calmly from a large glass full of beer. He wore glasses, and on the sides of his small head he had ears which were too big for his face. He was known as the Professor, and, when sitting next to him, Ossipon didn't feel very important. He stared at the Professor, wondering how to get from the little man the information that he wanted.

'Have you been out much today?' he said finally.

'No. I stayed in bed all the morning. Why?'

The Professor lived far away in a poor part of London where he rented a room in which, it seemed, mysterious things happened. His biggest piece of furniture was a very large cupboard which he kept locked at all times. He always stayed in his room when his **landlady** came to clean it and when he went out he always locked the door and took the key with him.

'Have you heard the news?' asked Ossipon.

The Professor shook his head. Ossipon waited for a moment and tried again.

'Tell me, do you give your **explosives** to anybody who asks for them?'

'Yes, why not?'

'Have you ever given any to a detective, for example?'

The little man smiled. He was very sure of himself. 'The police won't come near me.'

'But they could get the explosives from you and then arrest you.'

'I don't think so. They know what I always carry with me.' The Professor touched his coat lightly.

landlady a woman who gets money for renting out rooms

explosive something that explodes when you hit it or burn it

'Yes, enough explosive to kill yourself and everyone near you,' said Ossipon in a voice full of both wonder and fear.

'I always have my hand around the **rubber** ball inside my pocket. It **activates** the **detonator** inside the glass **jar**. The **tube** goes up here.' He quickly showed the brown rubber tube that disappeared into the inside pocket of his coat.

'Does it explode immediately?'

'No. It takes twenty seconds from the time I touch the ball.'

'Twenty seconds!' Ossipon couldn't believe it. 'That's terrible!'

'It is the weak part of this system. I am trying to **invent** something better. A really intelligent detonator.'

'Twenty seconds,' repeated Ossipon shaking his head.

'Nobody in this room could hope to escape,' said the little man looking around him.

Ossipon shook his head again as he pictured the terrible **destruction** of a bomb in that room. But the Professor went on talking calmly.

rubber made of soft, movable material

activate to make something work

detonator something that makes a bomb work

jar a glass container for food; for example, a jar of coffee

tube a long, narrow pipe

invent to think of something new or better

destruction when something is destroyed

'Other people believe that I will use my bomb. That's what makes me free. They need order and life. I need nothing but death – and that makes me strong.'

'Karl Yundt said something like that a short while ago.'

'Karl Yundt knows nothing. None of you people know anything.'

'But what do you want us to do?' asked Ossipon angrily.

'Invent the perfect detonator! That's what you should be thinking about. You aren't any better than the police. I met Inspector Heat the other day. He was thinking of so many things – his **boss**, his money, the newspapers – and you and your friends are the same as him. You talk and talk and you do nothing. I work fourteen hours a day inventing the perfect detonator. If necessary, I don't eat. And I work alone.'

Ossipon's face had gone red. 'Let's leave all that. What about the news, eh?' He took a newspaper out of his pocket. 'There was a bomb in Greenwich Park this morning at half-past ten. It left a big hole in the ground under a tree and there were pieces of a man's body all over the place. He **blew** himself **up**. Did you have anything to do with it?'

The Professor said 'Yes', almost smiling.

'I knew it!' cried Ossipon. 'You give your explosive to the first stupid person that asks!'

'Right! And why not? I don't take my orders from you! You aren't important enough.'

'Your detonator wasn't very good this time,' said Ossipon coldly. 'It killed the man.'

The Professor looked a little uncomfortable. 'Yes, well, someone has to try them.'

'Can't you describe the person you gave it to?'

'I can do more than just describe him. It was Verloc.'

'Verloc! Impossible.'

'Yes. Wasn't he an important man in your group?'

boss the person that you work for

blow up to explode

'Well, not really. He usually received comrades who were coming to England, but he wasn't really important. He had no ideas. Years ago, he used to speak at meetings in France, I believe, but he didn't do it very well. The police left him alone, I don't know why. He was married, you know. I suppose he started that shop with his wife's money. He seemed to do all right.'

Ossipon paused and spoke almost to himself: 'I wonder what that woman will do now?'

'Verloc told me that he wanted to destroy a building,' said the Professor. 'I gave him a thick glass jar full of explosive inside an old tin. Perhaps he activated the detonator and then forgot the time. He had twenty minutes. Or perhaps he dropped it. The detonator was fine, I'm sure.'

Ossipon was worried. 'All of this isn't very nice for me,' he said, as the Professor called the waiter and paid the bill. 'Karl has been ill in bed for a week and Michaelis is in the country writing a book. The police might get interested in me.'

'I don't know what happened to Verloc. It's a mystery,' said the Professor. 'But he's gone. The police know you did not help him.'

'I'm not so sure. But perhaps our friend Michaelis could support us when he speaks at one of our meetings. Michaelis is stupid, but people like him. And I could talk to a few newspapers.'

Ossipon thought about Verloc's shop in Brett Street. Were the police already there, asking questions? Then, he wondered how the police would **identify** Verloc after the bomb had done its violent work. Perhaps he was safe after all. Or perhaps not.

'What should I do now?' he said half to himself.

'Get what you can from the woman,' said the Professor, who had heard his words.

The little man finished his beer, got up and walked away from the table, and Ossipon, surprised at the Professor's words, sat alone for a little longer thinking. When he came out of the bar into the grey, dirty street, the Professor had already disappeared.

identify to say who someone is by name

READING CHECK

Tick the best answers.

a Why is Ossipon interested in talking to the Professor?
1 ☑ The Professor has some important information.
2 ☐ The Professor keeps explosives in his room.
3 ☐ The Professor is an anarchist.

b What does the Professor think about Ossipon and his political friends?
1 ☐ They are more intelligent than the police.
2 ☐ They have some interesting ideas.
3 ☐ They talk too much.

c Why don't the police arrest the Professor?
1 ☐ He always carries a bomb with him and is ready to use it.
2 ☐ He works alone.
3 ☐ He isn't dangerous.

d What happened in Greenwich Park?
1 ☐ A bomb destroyed Greenwich Observatory.
2 ☐ Someone left a bomb in a hole in the ground.
3 ☐ A bomb killed a man.

e Who did the Professor give the explosives to?
1 ☐ Michaelis.
2 ☐ Verloc.
3 ☐ Yundt.

f Why is Ossipon worried?
1 ☐ The police may not be able to identify Verloc's body.
2 ☐ The police may want to talk to him about the bomb.
3 ☐ The police may arrest Winnie Verloc.

WORD WORK

1 Match these words with the drawing of the Professor's bomb.

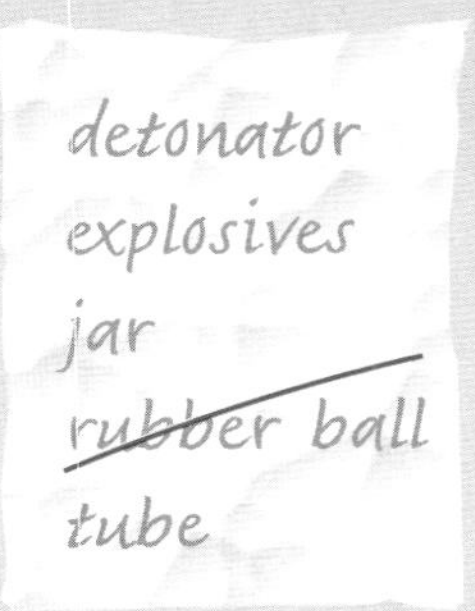

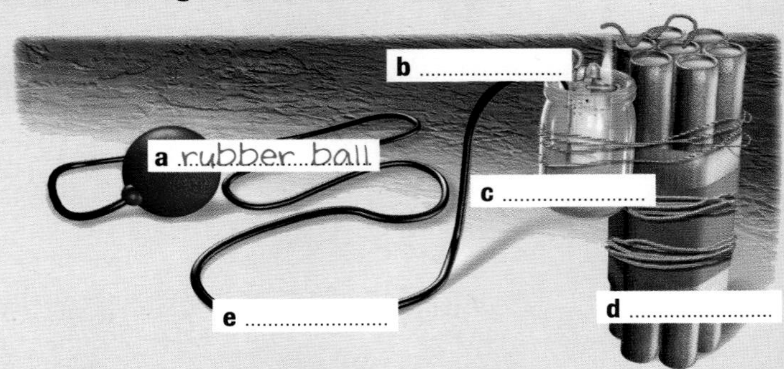

2 Complete the sentences with words from Chapter 3 in the correct form.

a The Professor keeps dangerous ..explosives.. in his cupboard.

b A man was killed when a bomb .... in Greenwich Park.

c The police will have problems .... his body.

d Chief Inspector Heat worries a lot about his ....

e The rubber ball in the Professor's coat pocket .... a detonator.

f The Professor would like to .... a new and better kind of bomb.

g The Professor stays in his room when his .... comes to clean it.

GUESS WHAT

In the next chapter we meet Chief Inspector Heat, the detective who is finding out about the bomb in Greenwich Park. What does he do? Tick the boxes.

a He meets … in the street.

1 ☐ the Professor
2 ☐ Ossipon
3 ☐ Stevie

b He talks to … about the bomb in the park.

1 ☐ an old woman selling flowers outside Greenwich Park
2 ☐ a policeman
3 ☐ Verloc

c He goes to see …

1 ☐ Michaelis.
2 ☐ Winnie Verloc.
3 ☐ his boss.

CHIEF INSPECTOR HEAT

Chief Inspector Heat

department a part of a large organization where people work

fog low, thick cloud that makes it difficult to see

shovel a metal thing that you use to dig and to pick things up with

THE Professor walked along the busy street. He felt the rubber ball in his left pocket and smiled to himself. He left the crowds and turned into a quiet, narrow street. A tall, well-built man was coming towards him. He stopped in surprise when he saw the Professor.

Chief Inspector Heat of the Special Crime **Department** had not had a good day. Just before eleven o'clock that morning, he had received news from Greenwich about the bomb. Less than a week before, he had told a very important person that the anarchists were not planning anything violent. The important man had believed him, and now Heat felt stupid. He had gone to the park and to the hospital where he had seen what was left of the body of the Greenwich bomber. It was impossible to identify. He then talked to the policeman who had arrived immediately after the bomb exploded.

'He's all there, sir. Every bit of him. I heard the bang and felt the ground shake. Then I saw a light through the **fog** and ran through the trees towards the Observatory.'

'You used a **shovel**,' said Heat, noticing some small stones among the pieces of body.

'Yes, I had to.'

Heat felt sick.

'An old woman saw two men coming out of the station,' said the policeman. 'One was tall and thin and carrying a tin. The other was fatter.' He looked at the body. 'Well, here's the tall, thin one. I suppose he fell over and the thing that he was carrying exploded.'

Heat picked up a piece of dark blue **cloth** with a narrow edge of blue **velvet**. The policeman spoke. 'The old woman noticed that. "A dark blue coat with a velvet **collar**," she said.'

Heat moved towards the window and looked interestedly at the cloth. Quickly, he pulled the cloth from the collar and put it in his pocket. Then he threw the piece of velvet back onto the table.

'Cover him up,' he ordered, and then he left. On the train back to town, Heat thought about his discovery. He wasn't going to say much about the man who had blown himself up.

When Inspector Heat met the Professor, he said to the little man, 'You are not wanted – yet. But when I want you I will know where to find you.'

'Well, if anything happens and we're both blown up, I suppose they will say nice things about you in the newspapers. Just think, they might **bury** us together!'

Heat was very angry, but he spoke quietly.

'I'll get you in the end.'

'I'm sure you will,' replied the Professor. 'But why not now? There's no one near us. It's the perfect chance.'

'Do you think I'm stupid? The law will win in the end. I don't know what your game is. I don't believe you know yourselves. Stop doing it – there are more of us than you.'

The Professor spoke more bravely than he felt: 'I am doing my job better than you're doing yours.'

'That's enough,' said Heat quickly.

The Professor laughed and continued on his way. He wanted to return to his lonely room as quickly as possible, far from the real world of the crowded city.

cloth clothes are made of this

velvet an expensive kind of cloth

collar the part of a coat that goes round the neck

bury to put a dead person under the ground

'The man's **mad**,' thought Heat as he watched the Professor leave. Now he had a more important problem to think about; what to say to his boss, the Assistant **Commissioner**.

The Assistant Commissioner was working at his desk. He had a foreign-looking face with dark hair and a dark beard. When Heat entered the room, he looked up.

'Ah, Heat. I suppose you were right when you said the London anarchists had nothing to do with this business. But we need to know who did it. Have you brought anything useful from Greenwich?'

Heat made his report. He explained that he believed two men had taken part in the bombing. One man had shown the other where to put the explosive and then left. He was probably waiting for the train when the bomb exploded.

The Assistant Commissioner watched Heat as he talked. He did not enjoy his job in London. He had begun working as a policeman abroad and he had liked it there. But then he had married while he was on holiday in England and his wife did not want to go abroad. She knew a lot of important people in England and this had helped him. But he hated working at his desk all day and he hated the English weather.

mad crazy

commissioner the most important person in a police department

'Are you looking for the other man?' he asked.

'Yes, sir. The porter at the station in Greenwich remembers them. The fat man was carrying a tin and he gave it to the thin young man in the station. This agrees with what the old woman told the police in Greenwich Park. And I saw bits of tin among the **remains** of the body.'

'And they caught the train to Greenwich? Two foreign anarchists going there from that small country station. That's strange.'

'It isn't so strange when you remember that Michaelis is staying in a **cottage** near the small country station.'

When the Assistant Commissioner heard the name 'Michaelis', he showed more interest in the case. The ex-prisoner was supported by a rich and important lady who was one of his wife's best friends. All kinds of people met at her house: kings, queens, artists, men of science, **politicians**, and even criminals.

Years before, Michaelis and some other men had tried to help some prisoners to escape from the police. The plan had gone wrong and one of the policemen was killed. Michaelis knew nothing about the shooting, but later he stupidly said he was sorry that the plan to help the prisoners had not worked. For that Michaelis was sent to prison for life. This made him famous. After fifteen years, he came out of prison on bail. Even after all the years in prison, he was still optimistic and continued to believe that people were naturally good. The Assistant Commissioner had been there when Michaelis first came to the great lady's house. She liked Michaelis a lot.

When he left she said, 'And that is what some people call a revolutionary! A good, kind man and they put him in prison for fifteen years. Now his parents and the girl he was going to marry are all dead. Someone will have to look after him.'

The Assistant Commissioner secretly agreed with the lady. Michaelis was strange, but not dangerous. 'If they send that man to prison again, she will never **forgive** me,' he thought.

remains what is left

cottage a small house in the country

politician a person who helps to make laws in a country

forgive (*past* **forgave**, **forgiven**) to stop being angry with someone for something bad that they did

READING CHECK

What happened on the day of the Greenwich bombing?
Put the parts of the summary in the correct order. Number them 1–6.

a ☐ A policeman heard the bang, saw a light, and ran to the Observatory. He picked up the pieces of the thin man's body to take them to the hospital.

b 1 An old woman saw two men – one thin, one fat – leaving Greenwich station. Soon after this the thin man fell over in the park and the bomb exploded.

c ☐ After talking with the Professor, Heat went to tell his boss, the Assistant Here he Commissioner, about the Greenwich bombing.

d ☐ Chief Inspector Heat left the hospital and went back to the centre of London. met the Professor by accident in the street and they talked.

e ☐ Chief Inspector Heat heard about the bomb and went to the Park. From there he went to the hospital to look at the dead man's body.

f ☐ At the hospital the policeman told Chief Inspector Heat that the thin man was wearing a dark blue coat. Chief Inspector Heat took a piece of the coat with him.

WORD WORK

1 Correct the boxed words in these sentences. They all come from Chapter 4.

a The young policeman sees a light through the **dog** in Greenwich Park.
........fog........

b The young policeman uses a **shaver** to pick up the pieces of the body.
....

c Chief Inspector Heat works for the Special Crime **Deportment** . ...

d Chief Inspector Heat picks up a piece of dark blue **broth** from the dead man's coat.
....

e Chief Inspector Heat puts a piece of the **dollar** in his pocket. ....

f The Professor laughs at the idea that people might **busy** him and Chief Inspector Heat together. ....

g Chief Inspector Heat thinks the Professor is **mud** . ...

2 Match the words in the sky with the underlined words in these sentences.

a The dead man was wearing a coat with a collar made of <u>an expensive kind of cloth</u>.
......velvet......

b It is impossible to identify the man from the <u>pieces that are left</u> of the dead body.
....

c Michaelis is living in a <u>small country house</u>. ....

d Michaelis goes to parties with <u>important people who make laws</u>. ....

e It is hard to <u>not be angry with</u> someone when they do something that you don't like.
....

f Chief Inspector Heat's boss is the Assistant <u>Head of a police department</u>.
....

GUESS WHAT

What happens in the next chapter? Tick the boxes.	**Yes**	**Perhaps**	**No**
a Chief Inspector Heat shows the piece of blue cloth to his boss.	☐	☐	☐
b Chief Inspector Heat tells his boss that Verloc is a spy.	☐	☐	☐
c Chief Inspector Heat finds out that Verloc is dead.	☐	☐	☐
d Chief Inspector Heat wants to arrest Michaelis.	☐	☐	☐
e The Assistant Commissioner decides to visit Verloc's shop.	☐	☐	☐
f The Assistant Commissioner speaks to his wife's friend about Michaelis.	☐	☐	☐

CHAPTER FIVE

The Assistant Commissioner visits Sir Ethelred

THE Assistant Commissioner turned to Heat. 'Do you have **proof** that Michaelis knows about this business?'

'Proof, sir? Yes, sir. **Trust** me.' Heat laughed as if he had a special secret.

'What did you find out at Greenwich?' asked the Assistant Commissioner.

Heat decided to be honest. 'I have an address, sir.' He showed his boss the piece of blue cloth that he had taken from among the remains of the body. 'This is from the coat worn by the man who blew himself up.' The Assistant Commissioner saw that there was an address hand-written on the cloth in ink.

'32 Brett Street. What's that?'

'It's a shop, sir.' Heat explained about Verloc.

'Does anyone **else** know about Verloc?'

'No, sir. A personal friend in the French police told me he was an Embassy spy. It was **private** information.'

'And how long have you known this spy?'

'I first saw him seven years ago, when some important foreign visitors were on a visit here. Baron Stott-Wartenheim was Ambassador then. He sent for me and he told me that a man had come from Paris with some important information. He showed me into another room where a large man was waiting. The light was not good and I could not see him well. We talked and he gave me some news that probably saved us from some serious problems on the day of the important visit.

'I saw the large man, Verloc, again some time later in the street. One of our detectives watched him for a few days and he told me that the man had married his landlady's daughter. They had gone on holiday and he had seen some old Paris **labels** on their bags.

proof information that shows that something is really true

trust to believe that someone is honest and good

else more or extra

private for one person or for very few people to know

label a piece of paper or cloth that you fix to something to give information about it

When I went to Paris for work, I spoke to my friend in the police there. He told me that the man worked with an international group of revolutionaries. He said that he was now a secret agent of one of the foreign Embassies in London. At last I had proof that he was the man whom I had seen at Baron Stott-Wartenheim's.

'One night, I went to his shop and I spoke to him. I said that the police would leave him alone if he did nothing too bad. This was useful to him, because some of the things that he sells have to go through **Customs** at Dover.'

'And what do you get from him in return for not speaking to Customs?'

'Our men take careful notice of anybody that they see with him. I can always get an address from him. I usually write him a note, **unsigned**, and he answers me in the same way with an unsigned note sent to my private address. If I think something is going to happen, he can usually tell me something about it.'

'He didn't tell you anything this time.'

'I didn't ask. He isn't one of our men. We don't pay him.'

'No. He's a spy paid by a foreign country!'

'I must be free to work in my own way, sir. There are things that not everyone should know.'

'Not even me?' said the Assistant Commissioner angrily. Heat said nothing, so he continued. 'Is the house watched by the police?'

'Not all the time. I don't think that Verloc knows anything about this Greenwich business.'

'No? Then how do you explain this?' The Assistant Commissioner looked at the piece of blue cloth lying on the table.

'I can't explain it, sir. I think that the man who knows the most about all this is probably Michaelis.'

'What about the other man who escaped from the park?'

'I think he will be far away by now.'

Suddenly the Assistant Commissioner was in a hurry to end the conversation and he told the Chief Inspector to meet him early

customs a special office that checks people and luggage coming into or leaving a country

unsigned with no name written on it

the next morning. Soon after Heat had gone, his boss put on his hat and left the building. He had decided to speak about what he knew to a very important politician – Sir Ethelred, the **Home Secretary**. He hurried towards the **Parliament** buildings.

The Home Secretary was a big, white-faced man. Next to him, the Assistant Commissioner looked small and dark and even more foreign-looking. Sir Ethelred spoke in a loud voice.

'Now, don't give me any **details**. I don't have time for that. But I would like to know if this is the beginning of more problems from the anarchists.'

'I don't think so, sir.'

'Hah! Less than a month ago, I was told that nothing like this was even possible.'

'I'm sorry, sir, but it wasn't me who told you that.'

'That's true. It was Heat. You haven't been in the new job long, have you? How are things?'

'I believe I'm learning something new every day, Sir Ethelred. I want to talk to you about the Greenwich bombing.'

'Very well. Go ahead.'

Home Secretary a very important politician; the head of the police in England

Parliament the group of politicians that make and change the laws of a country

detail one fact or piece of information

The Assistant Commissioner talked for some minutes and Sir Ethelred listened carefully.

'So you see, sir,' finished the Assistant Commissioner, 'this is special.'

'You are right. To think that the Ambassador of a foreign country is doing things like that! Really, these people are impossible! What should we do, do you think?'

'We shouldn't accept these secret agents, sir. They are dangerous. And perhaps we should take Heat off the job ...'

'What! Heat? Not very clever, eh?' said Sir Ethelred who did not like the Chief Inspector.

'I couldn't say that, sir. He's the best in his department. All my information is from him. But I've discovered that Heat has been using Verloc privately and I don't agree with that. It's a good idea to stop Verloc, but Heat may see this as a personal **attack**. I believe that I can find out what is behind the Greenwich business if I go myself to the shop in Brett Street.'

'Why can't Heat go?'

'Because I want to know the real story behind the bombing and he just wants to arrest as many well-known anarchists as possible. Verloc will help. It won't be difficult to frighten him. Can I tell him that he will be safe if he helps us?'

'Of course. Question him and find out as much as you can. Come to Parliament later tonight and tell us what you know.'

Happily the Assistant Commissioner returned to his office where he changed from his normal clothes and put on a short coat and a low, round hat. Then he went into the street.

It was dark and raining. He took a **cab** to a small Italian restaurant where he sat alone at one of the side tables. When he saw himself in one of the mirrors, he pulled up the collar of his coat so that it partly covered his thin, dark face. 'That's better,' he thought.

Brett Street was not far, and the Assistant Commissioner was soon walking towards Mr Verloc's shop.

attack a fight or strong disagreement with someone

cab a kind of car pulled by a horse

ACTIVITIES

READING CHECK

Correct the mistakes in these sentences.

a Chief Inspector Heat shows the name from the blue coat collar to the Assistant Commissioner.

b Number 32 Brett Street is Michaelis's address.

c Heat first met Verloc in Paris when Baron Stott-Wartenheim was Ambassador.

d A personal friend in the British police told Heat that Verloc was a spy.

e Verloc gives information to Heat from time to time and so he's left alone by the Embassy.

f Heat says that the police are watching Verloc's shop all the time.

g Heat thinks that Verloc is the man who knows the most about the Greenwich bomb.

h After Heat leaves, the Assistant Commissioner walks slowly to see Sir Ethelred.

i Sir Ethelred agrees that the Assistant Commissioner must arrest Verloc.

j The Assistant Commissioner visits Verloc's shop before going to an Italian restaurant.

WORD WORK

Find words in the hats to complete the sentences.

a The Assistant Commissioner changes his clothes and takes a c_ _ to a restaurant in Soho.

b The Assistant Commissioner asks Heat for some clear p_ _ _ _ that Michaelis knows about the Greenwich bomb.

c Heat didn't tell anyone that Verloc was an Embassy spy because it was p_ _ _ _ _ _ _ information. (v a i t r p e)

d The Paris l_ _ _ _ _ on the Verloc's travelling bags helped Heat to identify Verloc as the spy he'd met before. (s a l l e b)

e The C_ _ _ _ _ _ _ officers in Dover don't look closely at the boxes of magazines that Mr Verloc buys from abroad for his shop. (u m t s o c s)

f Heat and Verloc send each other u_ _ _ _ _ _ _ notes because they don't want anyone who finds the notes to identify them as the writers. (d e i n n g u s)

g The Assistant Commissioner goes to see Sir Ethelred in his office in one of the p_ _ _ _ _ _ _ _ _ _ buildings. (a l t a e n p m i r)

h Sir Ethelred is the H_ _ _ S_ _ _ _ _ _ _ _ _; it's his job to look after the police in the whole of England. (m h e o t e r r a s e c y)

i In 1886, many politicians were worried about a_ _ _ _ _ _ _ by anarchists and revolutionaries. (t a k a s c t)

j Sir Ethelred doesn't have time to listen to lots of d_ _ _ _ _ _ _ of the story; he just wants the important facts. (e l a s d i t)

k The Assistant Commissioner doesn't really t_ _ _ _ _ Heat to find out the real story from Verloc. (u s r t t)

GUESS WHAT

What do you think happens in the next chapter? Tick three sentences.

a ☐ The story goes back to a day some time before the Greenwich bombing.
b ☐ The story goes forward to a time after the police have caught the bomber.
c ☐ Winnie's mother decides to leave Verloc's house.
d ☐ Verloc tells Winnie about his problems with the Embassy.
e ☐ Verloc tells Winnie that he is going abroad for some time.

CHAPTER SIX

Winnie's mother moves out

ONE day, between Verloc's visit to the Embassy and the Greenwich bombing, Winnie's mother moved out. She had managed to get a little **charity** cottage from the people that her husband had worked for. Winnie was so surprised when she heard the news that she stopped cleaning the back room and stared at her mother.

'Why did you want to do that, Mother? Weren't you comfortable enough here?'

The old woman explained how 'poor daddy's friends' had helped her to get the house. When the story was finished, Winnie left the room. Her mother was **glad** that there were no more questions. The day before she left Brett Street, she said to Winnie: 'Everything I leave here is yours now, my dear.' She left nothing for Stevie because she thought it was best if the boy had to **depend on** Verloc. If Stevie had nothing, they could not leave him to look after himself.

On the day that she left, an old cab, pulled by an even older horse, came to take Winnie's mother to her new house. The two women got into the cab and Stevie climbed onto the **box** next to the driver.

They started their journey through the grey streets. The horse was old and thin and it went very slowly, although the driver **whipped** it from time to time.

Up on the box, Stevie was worried. 'You m-m-mustn't w-w-whip,' he said, stuttering, to the driver. 'It h-h-hurts.'

The driver looked at him, and he whipped the horse again; not because he was a bad man, but because it was what he usually did and he saw nothing wrong in it.

It was all too much for Stevie. Suddenly, he stood up and, stuttering more than ever, he jumped down from the box. There

charity given to poor people for little or no money

glad happy

depend on to need someone's help in order to live

box the place on top of a cab where people can sit

whip to hit with a special long, thin stick

were shouts from the people in the street as the angry driver stopped his cab suddenly. Winnie put her head out of the window and her mother shouted, 'Is the boy hurt?'

Stevie was not hurt, but he was excited. 'We're t-t-too heavy.' he stuttered.

'Stevie! Get up on the box now, and don't try to get down again.' Winnie's voice shook a little.

'No. I m-m-must w-w-walk.'

'Mr Verloc won't be happy at all about this, Stevie.'

The name of Winnie's husband calmed Stevie down a little. Unhappily, he climbed up again onto the box.

'Don't do that again, do you hear?' said the driver. He did not speak too angrily because he was beginning to realize that Stevie was not the same as other young men.

The cab continued on its way and for a while, the only sound was that of the horse's feet on the hard road. Inside the cab, Winnie said; 'You've done what you wanted, Mother, but do you think you'll be happy?'

The old woman tried to be optimistic and said; 'I know you'll visit me as often as you can, won't you dear?'

'Of course,' said Winnie.

'And I must see that poor boy every Sunday.' She thought of the journey that Stevie now had to make to get to her cottage from the shop and all her optimistic thoughts disappeared. He had to take two buses! It was going to be too difficult for him! She started to cry.

'Don't cry, Mother. I can't come myself every week, but I'll make sure that he doesn't get lost.'

'Here you are!' said the driver.

The cab had stopped outside one of a group of little low cottages. The old woman got out with a key in her hand and Winnie paid the driver. Stevie helped his mother to take her things into the house. Then he came out and stared with a worried look at the horse. The driver spoke to him.

'Don't worry about the horse, son. What about me, eh? I work until three or four in the morning. I get cold and hungry. And I've got a wife and four children at home. This isn't an easy world.'

'Bad!' agreed Stevie. He felt sorry for the horse, and for the driver with the wife and four children at home, too. He hated the unfairness of it all.

The driver walked away pulling his horse and cab after him. Stevie watched them go with his mouth open. He was sorry and angry at the same time. When he felt like this, he did not know what to do. Winnie came out of the house and took his arm. She did not really understand her brother's feelings, but she knew that she must make him think of something else.

'Now Stevie, you must look after me when we cross the road, and you get onto the bus first, like a good brother.'

This worked well. Being a good brother was the most important thing in the world to Stevie.

They walked down the poor, badly-lit street. The old horse with its cab was standing with its head down outside a pub.

'Poor thing,' said Winnie without thinking.

'Poor! Poor!' agreed Stevie. 'The driver is poor, too. He told me himself.'

'Come on, Stevie. You can't help that.'

Stevie thought for a while. 'Bad world for poor people.'

'Nobody can help that.'

She looked at him with great **affection**. 'Quick, Stevie. Stop that green bus.' Stevie, feeling important, lifted up his arm. The bus stopped and they got on.

An hour later they arrived home. Verloc was there, reading the newspaper. He stared heavily at his wife, but said nothing and showed no interest in what they had done that day.

At supper-time, Winnie called to her husband as usual, 'Adolf', and, without a word, Verloc came to the table where he ate in silence. Winnie noticed the empty place where her mother usually sat and realized that she missed her very much. She looked at her husband. 'Are you going out tonight?'

Verloc shook his head, but two minutes later he got up and left. He did not know who he could find to plant a bomb at Greenwich Observatory, but the streets and the crowded bars held no answers for him. Feeling worse than before, he finally returned home, where he locked the front door and went straight upstairs.

Winnie was already in bed, but she was not sleeping. Verloc's heavy silence was beginning to worry her. As usual when she was worried she talked about something else.

'Mother's done what she wanted to do. But I don't understand it. I don't know what I am going to do to make Stevie feel happy. He'll be worried about her for days.'

Verloc got into bed. He really wanted to tell his wife everything about his problems with the Embassy, but instead he said: 'I am going abroad tomorrow. I'll be away for a week, or perhaps two. Will you be all right?'

Winnie said, 'I shall manage with Stevie's help.'

affection a feeling of love

ACTIVITIES

READING CHECK

Match the first and second parts of these sentences.

a Winnie cannot understand why her mother ...
b Winnie's mother leaves nothing for Stevie because she ...
c Stevie jumps down from the cab because he ...
d Winnie's mother cries because Stevie ...
e Stevie is angry because he ...
f That evening Winnie realizes that she ...
g After supper, Verloc ...
h When Winnie is worried about things she usually ...
i Instead of telling Winnie about his problems, Verloc ...

1 talks about something else.
2 misses her mother very much.
3 wants to move.
4 doesn't like to see the driver hurting the horse.
5 decides to go abroad.
6 thinks the world is unfair.
7 wants Verloc to feel that he must look after the boy.
8 will find it hard to come and visit her.
9 goes out to find someone to plant the bomb.

WORD WORK

Find words in the wheel of the cab to complete the sentences on page 39.

a Stevie doesn't like it when the cab driver ....whips.... his horse.

b Stevie sits up high on the .... next to the cab driver.

c The people Winnie's father used to work for give Winnie's mother a .... house to live in.

d Stevie is .... to stop a bus for Winnie when she asks him to.

e Winnie feels great .... for her younger brother.

f Winnie's mother thinks that it's better for Stevie to .... on Verloc than to have to look after himself.

GUESS WHAT

What happens in the next chapter? Match the pictures and the sentences.

VERLOC

STEVIE

WINNIE

THE ASSISTANT COMMISSIONER

CHIEF INSPECTOR HEAT

a .... comes home after some time abroad.

b .... puts Verloc's hat and bag away when he comes in.

c .... is happy when Verloc takes Stevie out with him.

d .... goes to stay with Michaelis for a while.

e .... comes back home late on the day of the Greenwich bomb.

f .... comes to the shop and takes Verloc away to talk to him.

g .... comes to the shop and shows Winnie the address from the blue coat.

Verloc takes Stevie with him

AFTER ten days, Verloc returned from his journey abroad. Looking very tired, he walked heavily into the shop, dropped his bag on the floor, and fell into the chair. Stevie picked up the bag so quickly that Verloc looked at him in surprise.

Verloc was not hungry, but he did not refuse the food that Winnie put in front of him. In silence, he listened while Winnie told him the news.

'Stevie's been difficult to manage. But he's still working hard and helping in the house. He can't do enough for us.'

At that moment, Stevie picked up Verloc's hat and took it away carefully with the bag into the kitchen. For the second time that day, Verloc was surprised.

'You can do anything with that boy, Adolf. He'll go through fire for you, if you ask him to,' said Winnie, smiling.

Verloc spent most of the day sleeping in front of the fire. In the afternoon, he said he was going for a walk.

Winnie said, 'Why don't you take Stevie with you, Adolf?'

'Yes, all right. But perhaps he'll walk away from me and get lost in the street.'

Winnie shook her head.

'He won't. You don't know him. That boy thinks too much of you. But don't worry. If he gets lost, he'll soon arrive home safely.'

'All right,' Verloc said, trusting his wife.

Winnie watched the two men with something like affection as they walked down the street, one short and heavy, the other tall and thin. The cloth of their coats was the same and their hats were round and black. 'They could be father and son,' she said to herself happily.

In the days that followed, Verloc took Stevie out more and more

often, but the boy had started to talk to himself and seemed angry. Winnie was afraid that he was listening to her husband's friends too much. Verloc said that he might calm down if he went to stay with Michaelis in the country. Winnie soon agreed. After all, Michaelis was always so kind to Stevie, not like some of the others, and he seemed to like the boy.

So Verloc took Stevie away the next day. When Winnie told Stevie not to get his clothes dirty in the country, he did not look at her in his usual trusting way. She smiled at him.

'Don't look at me like that. You know you get very untidy sometimes, Stevie.'

Some days later, on the evening of the Greenwich bombing, Verloc did not come back until it was almost dark. Winnie had been alone all day. She was sitting **sewing** when the cracked bell rang and Verloc came in with his head down and went straight towards the back room.

sew to join or fix pieces of cloth together

'What an awful day,' said Winnie calmly. 'Have you been to see Stevie?'

'No, I haven't,' said Verloc softly and he banged the door shut loudly behind him.

Winnie sat still for some time without touching her sewing. Then she got up to light the gas. It was time to make tea.

As she went through the back room on her way to the kitchen, she heard a strange **rattling** noise that made her stop in surprise and fear.

Verloc had pulled a chair towards the fireplace and was sitting almost on top of the fire with his head in his hands. The sound Winnie had heard was made by his teeth which were rattling violently. At the same time, his **huge** back was shaking.

'Where have you been today?' Winnie asked.

'Nowhere,' answered Verloc in a low, **hoarse** voice. Then, realizing that this was not enough, he added, 'I've been to the bank to take out all the money. We may need it soon.'

'I don't know what you mean.' Winnie spoke calmly, but she did not move from where she stood.

'You know you can trust me,' said Verloc hoarsely.

Winnie turned slowly towards the cupboard saying, 'Oh, yes, I can trust you.' She put the plates, the bread, and the butter on the table. Then, remembering that her husband had been out all day and was probably hungry, she went to the cupboard again for the cold meat and the carving knife and fork. She called quietly to Verloc, who seemed to be asleep, 'Adolf.'

Verloc got up and **staggered** a little before he sat down at the table. He did not touch the meat, but drank three cups of tea. His eyes and face were red, and his hair was standing up. Winnie said at last, 'Take your shoes off. Your feet are sure to be wet, and you aren't going out any more this evening.'

Verloc told Winnie that he was thinking of going to live abroad, perhaps to France or California.

'What an idea!' said Winnie. 'You can't be serious. You've got

rattle to make a noise like something hard being hit again and again

huge very big

hoarse losing your voice

stagger to walk badly and almost fall

a good business and a comfortable home. And you aren't tired of me.' She got up and walked to the other end of the table. Resting on Verloc's shoulder from behind, she **kissed** his head and waited there for a moment. Finally she said, 'If you go abroad, you'll have to go without me.' She was thinking about Stevie. 'And then you'll miss me. So you know you couldn't do that.'

'Of course not,' said Verloc in a louder voice. At that moment, the shop bell rang.

'Shop, Adolf. You go.'

Verloc slowly went towards the shop.

When he came in again a few minutes later, his face had changed from red to white.

'I have to go out this evening after all,' he said, but he didn't move to pick up his coat.

Without a word, Winnie walked into the shop and closed the door behind her. The man waiting there was thin and dark and looked foreign. He smiled at Winnie and she said, 'If you need somewhere to stay, the Continental Hotel is a good place. My husband will take you there.'

'A good idea,' said the thin man whose smiling face had suddenly become hard.

Winnie returned to the back room and spoke to her husband.

'Adolf, that man isn't one of those Embassy people, is he?'

Verloc jumped in surprise and fear. 'Who's been talking to you about Embassy people?'

'You have. In your sleep. I didn't really understand what you were saying, but I knew that something was worrying you.'

Verloc was red-faced and angry. 'I could cut their hearts out! But they'll have to be careful. I've got a tongue in my head.'

'Well, get rid of that man and come home to me. You're not well. But before you go, perhaps you should give me the money that you took out of the bank.'

'Oh yes! Yes. Here it is.' Verloc gave his wife a wallet full of notes which she hid inside her dress.

kiss to touch lovingly with your lips

Shortly after Verloc had left, the cracked bell rang again. This time, it was Chief Inspector Heat who had come for some 'private' information. Winnie told him that her husband had gone out.

'I think that you know who I am. My name is Chief Inspector Heat of the Special Crimes Department. Did your husband say when he would be back?'

'He wasn't alone.' Winnie described the dark stranger and Heat recognized the Assistant Commissioner and sighed. He decided to find out how much Winnie knew.

'What do you know about the Greenwich bombing?'

Winnie told him that she knew nothing.

'Oh, and there's another thing,' said Heat. 'I've got a coat here, probably stolen, and I think it came from here. Your address is on it in purple ink. I see you have a lot of ink here,' said Heat looking at the lines of small bottles standing ready for someone to buy them.

'That's my brother's coat, then. I wrote that address myself. He's been staying with our friend Michaelis in the country.'

Heat almost laughed. 'Right. And is your brother a large, heavy man?'

'Oh no. That must be the thief. Stevie's tall and thin.'

Heat put his hand in his pocket and pulled out a newspaper and a piece of blue cloth. He gave the cloth to Winnie.

'I suppose you recognize this?'

Winnie's eyes seemed to grow bigger as she took it in her hands. 'Yes,' she whispered and staggered backwards a little. 'But why is it pulled out of the coat like this?'

At that moment, Heat began to realize the extraordinary true facts of the Greenwich bombing. Verloc was 'the other man'!

Winnie had sat down suddenly and was staring in front of her. She did not look up when the bell rang and Verloc came in alone. He walked up to Heat, led him into the back room, and closed the door behind them.

Winnie ran to the door and fell onto her knees with her ear to the keyhole. She could hear Heat's voice clearly.

'You are the other man, Verloc. Two men entered the park.'

'Then arrest me now.'

'Oh, no. I know you've been talking to my boss. He'll have to manage this little business all by himself. But just remember, it was me who found out the true story.'

Winnie heard her husband say, 'I never noticed that she had done that', and she knew that he was looking at the coat label.

Now Heat was speaking again. 'How did you get away?'

'I was walking away when I heard the bomb explode. It came too soon and I started running through the fog. No one saw me until I was past the end of George Street.'

Winnie tried to put her ear closer to the keyhole. Her lips were blue and her hands were as cold as ice.

Heat spoke again. 'We think he **tripped** over a tree **root**. He was blown up into little bits. They had to pick him up with a shovel.'

Winnie got up and staggered towards the chair. She picked up the newspaper that Heat had left there earlier and tried to open it, but failed. Finally, she threw it on the floor. On the other side of the door Heat said, 'What made you do it?'

Thinking of Vladimir, Verloc replied, 'A real pig made me do it, a gentleman!'

Heat opened the door and walked past Winnie into the street. She heard the bell, but she did not look up. Instead she put her hands over her face. In the dark little shop, the only brightness came from the gold wedding ring on Winnie's left hand which shone brightly in the darkness.

trip to hit your foot against something so that you fall or nearly fall

root the part of a plant that grows under the ground

READING CHECK

Correct nine more mistakes in the chapter summary.

Verloc comes home after a journey abroad and finds Stevie is ~~unhelpful~~ helpful around the house.

Verloc starts to take Winnie with him when he goes out.

After some days of going out walking together, Verloc starts talking to himself angrily.

Winnie is worried. Verloc takes Stevie away to Winnie's mother's house in order for him to calm down.

The day of the Greenwich bombing, Verloc comes home early. He has lots of money with him and talks of going abroad. Winnie brings him food.

Then the Home Secretary visits the shop. Verloc gives Winnie all his money and leaves to talk with his visitor.

Soon after, Chief Inspector Heat arrives and asks Winnie what she knows of the Greenwich bombing. She says she knows everything.

When he shows her the address on the piece of blue cloth, she tells him it comes from her husband's coat. Heat realizes that Stevie was the 'Greenwich bomber' and Verloc was the 'other man'.

When Verloc comes back home alone, he and Heat talk together privately and Winnie listens at the window. After some time Verloc walks past Winnie out into the street.

Winnie covers her face with her hands.

ACTIVITIES

WORD WORK

Correct the boxed words in these sentences.

a Winnie Verloc likes to **new** and mend clothes in the evening. ....sew.......

b She hears Verloc's teeth **battling** in the room next door. ....

c Verloc has a **hugs** back. ....

d His voice is very **coarse** because he's cried a lot, and it's hard to hear him now. ....

e His legs were weak and so he **stammered** when he got up. ....

f Winnie puts her lips on the top of Verloc's head and **misses** him there. ....

g Heat and his men think that Stevie **trapped** over something and fell. ....

h One of the tree **boots** in Greenwich Park made Stevie fall. ....

GUESS WHAT

What do you think happens in the next chapter? Tick the boxes.

a ☐ The Assistant Commissioner / ☐ Chief Inspector Heat tells Sir Ethelred who the 'Greenwich bomber' was.

b The Assistant Commissioner tells his wife's friend that Michaelis

☐ planned the Greenwich bomb attack.

☐ is out of trouble.

c The Assistant Commissioner meets Mr Vladimir at ☐ the Embassy. / ☐ a party.

d Mr Vladimir says that the British police ☐ aren't hard enough on criminals. / ☐ are wonderful.

e The Assistant Commissioner tells Mr Vladimir he knows that ☐ Verloc / ☐ Michaelis is a secret agent.

f Mr Vladimir ☐ is / ☐ isn't surprised when he hears that the British police know who the Greenwich bomber was.

The Assistant Commissioner meets Vladimir

THE Assistant Commissioner was driven quickly in a cab from Brett Street to Westminster where he got out at the entrance to the Houses of Parliament. He was shown immediately into a poorly-lit room where the greenish-coloured **lamps** gave the feeling of being in a forest. The Home Secretary was sitting behind a large, almost empty desk. Through the green shadows the Assistant Commissioner could only see a heavy head resting on a large, white hand. He sat down at the other side of the desk. In the green light, he looked darker and more foreign than ever.

Sir Ethelred showed no surprise at the other man's early arrival, but he wanted to know the news and his voice was hard. 'Well,' he said, 'what have you found out?'

'Verloc was very quick to tell me everything, sir. His brother-in-law, nothing more than a weak boy, was the person who was killed. Another interesting thing is that I'm sure Michaelis had nothing to do with it although the boy had been staying with him. It's difficult to believe, but Verloc was **terrified** of that man Vladimir. He thought that he and the other Embassy people would destroy his life. I don't think he planned the death of that poor boy, but he completely lost his head.'

Something moved among the green shadows of the room and the great man spoke.

'What have you done with him?'

'I let him go, Sir Ethelred. I don't think he will disappear. He seemed to want to be with his wife. He has to think of the possible danger from his comrades, too. How will he explain trying to disappear to them?'

The great man, who perhaps had other, more important things to think about, got up heavily.

lamp something that gives light

terrified very frightened

'Tonight I will discuss what to do with Verloc and I'll send for you tomorrow morning.' He held out his big, white hand and shook the thin, dark hand of the Assistant Commissioner. He had his information and the conversation was over.

The Assistant Commissioner walked home and changed his clothes. There was time after all to visit his wife's friend, the great lady who looked after Michaelis. He was glad – he knew that he was always welcome in her house.

When he entered the large and crowded room, he saw his wife talking to a small group of people in the corner. The great lady herself was sitting talking to a man with a thin face and a short beard. She **greeted** the Assistant Commissioner warmly.

'I never hoped to see you here tonight. Annie told me that you were working.'

'Yes, I had no idea myself that my work would be over so soon.' He spoke in a lower voice: 'I am glad to tell you that Michaelis is out of trouble now.'

A silence fell. The other man smiled a little and the lady said: 'I don't know if you have ever met before.'

Mr Vladimir and the Assistant Commissioner were introduced and greeted each other politely. It was surprising how, sooner or later, everybody came to this house. Another woman standing next to them turned and spoke now, looking towards Vladimir: 'He's been frightening me with all his talk about Greenwich. He says we must stop these people or the future is black for us.'

'Oh, Mr Vladimir is good at frightening people,' said the Assistant Commissioner. 'But I'm sure he knows the true **importance** of what happened at Greenwich.'

Vladimir did not trust policemen and he trusted this one less than most. What did the man mean with his talk of 'importance'? He smiled when he answered, but his eyes were hard.

'Perhaps we have problems in my country because you let these people do what they like in your country.'

greet to say 'hello' to someone

importance valuable meaning of something

furious very angry

Vladimir got up to leave and, when he had turned away, the Assistant Commissioner got up, too.

'I thought you were going to stay and take Annie home,' said the great lady.

'I still have a little work to do. It may be important.'

The Assistant Commissioner went out into the street first and Vladimir waited as long as possible before he did the same. But it was not long enough. The policeman was still standing there and he started to walk along the street next to the other man. Vladimir was **furious** – what did he want?

'Terrible weather,' said Vladimir angrily.

'But not too cold,' replied the Assistant Commissioner. Then he added, 'We've got a man called Verloc helping us. I think that you know him.'

'What makes you say that?'

'I don't. It's Verloc who says that.'

'A lying dog of some kind,' said Vladimir, surprised that the English police could be so clever.

'Now we can really begin to get rid of all foreign spies from this country. We can't catch them one by one. The only way is to make things difficult for the people who employ them. The arrest of this man Verloc will show people how dangerous they are.'

'Nobody will believe what a man like that says.'

'I think that they will believe him when they hear the full story.'

'But you're just making things easier for anyone who wants to call himself a revolutionary,' cried Vladimir.

'Look, we have enough work to do catching the real revolutionaries. The last thing we want is to spend our time running after **fake** ones.'

'I can't agree with you. What you want to do is terrible. We should be good Europeans, not just look after our own interests.'

'Yes,' said the Assistant Commissioner. 'Except that you look at Europe from the other end. No foreign country can **complain** about our police this time. In less than twelve hours we have identified the dead man, discovered who planned the bombing, and found out who had the idea in the first place. And we can go further, but we will stop inside our own country.'

'So you know that this crime was planned abroad?' said Vladimir quickly.

'Well, in a way,' said the Assistant Commissioner. 'But that's a detail. I'm talking to you because it's your country that complains most about our police. As you can see, we are not always so bad.'

'Thank you for telling me,' said Vladimir through his teeth.

'We know every anarchist here, and where they are,' said the Assistant Commissioner, sounding just like Inspector Heat. 'All we need to do now to make everything safe is to get rid of the secret agent.'

Vladimir had heard more than enough. Without a word, he stopped a passing cab, jumped inside and drove off.

The Assistant Commissioner looked at his watch and saw that it was only half-past ten. Smiling to himself, he thought that he had had a very full evening.

fake not real

complain to say that you are unhappy or angry about something

READING CHECK

1 What do they say? Complete the sentences.

1 'Annie told me that you were working,'

2 'We've got a man called Verloc helping us.'

3 'Nobody will believe what a man like that says,'

4 'I'm glad to tell you that Michaelis is out of trouble,'

5 'Verloc was quick to tell me everything,'

6 'I will tell you what to do about Verloc tomorrow.'

a 'Verloc was quick to tell me everything,' says the Assistant Commissioner to Sir Ethelred.

b Sir Ethelred tells the Assistant Commissioner, ...

c .... says the great lady to the Assistant Commissioner.

d .... says the Assistant Commissioner to the great lady.

e The Assistant Commissioner says to Mr Vladimir, ...

f .... replies Mr Vladimir to the Assistant Commissioner.

2 Are these sentences true or false? Tick the boxes.

	True	False
a Verloc told the Assistant Commissioner everything about the Greenwich bombing.	✔	☐
b Sir Ethelred tells the Assistant Commissioner to arrest Verloc.	☐	☐
c The Assistant Commissioner meets Mr Vladimir for the first time at the great lady's party.	☐	☐
d The Assistant Commissioner knows who planned the Greenwich bombing.	☐	☐
e Mr Vladimir enjoys talking to the Assistant Commissioner.	☐	☐

WORD WORK

Find words in the puzzle and complete the sentences.

a Annie's rich lady friend ...greets.... the Assistant Commissioner when he arrives at the party in her house.

b Mr Vladimir always .... about the British police.

c There are green .... in Sir Ethelred's office.

d The true .... of the Greenwich Park bombing for the Assistant Commissioner is that he knows Mr Vladimir told Verloc to do it.

e Mr Vladimir is .... when he realizes that the Assistant Commissioner wants to talk to him privately.

f Verloc obeys Mr Vladimir because he is .... of him.

GUESS WHAT

What happens in the next chapter? Tick two sentences for each person.

Verloc ...

a ☐ tells Winnie that he didn't want to hurt Stevie.

b ☐ is angry with Winnie for putting the label in Stevie's coat.

c ☐ kisses Winnie and takes her in his arms lovingly.

d ☐ decides to leave Winnie and never come back.

e ☐ eats something and lies down on the sofa.

Winnie ...

a ☐ tells Verloc she loves him and forgives him.

b ☐ says she never wants to look at Verloc again.

c ☐ cries a lot about Stevie dying.

d ☐ kills Verloc with the carving knife.

e ☐ goes off alone to her mother's house.

CHAPTER NINE

Winnie and Verloc

AFTER Chief Inspector Heat had left, Verloc walked into the shop, wondering what to say to Winnie. She had not moved and she still had her hands over her face. When he spoke at last, her body began to shake.

'Winnie, you know that I didn't want anything to happen to Stevie. Heat was stupid, telling you so suddenly like that, eh?'

When Winnie did not reply, Verloc thought that he should leave her alone for a while. He went into the back room where the food still lay on the table. Taking off his hat, he put it down lazily on the table itself. Then, taking hold of the carving knife, he cut himself a piece of bread and meat.

He had not eaten all day. There was no food in Michaelis's cottage. When Michaelis had sat down that morning to write his book, Verloc had called up the stairs, 'I'm taking this young man home for a day or two.' He had not waited for an answer, but had left the house quickly, followed by Stevie. Now that his busy day was over, Verloc felt very empty. He ate standing up and tried to make Winnie talk to him.

'Come on, Winnie. We've got to think of tomorrow. You will have to be strong after I am taken away.'

Winnie's body was shaking more than ever. Verloc felt sorry for his wife, but he really had no idea of how she felt about Stevie. He had never understood much about Winnie.

'You should look at me when I'm talking to you, Winnie.'

Winnie's voice was flat and dead-sounding: 'I never want to look at you as long as I live.'

'Come on, Winnie. You can't sit here in the shop. Someone may come in. This won't bring him back. At least you haven't lost me, have you?'

Winnie sat without moving or speaking, and Verloc began

to feel afraid. He tried to take hold of her wrist, but she suddenly jumped up and ran away from him into the kitchen. She had not looked at him once.

Verloc sat down on the empty chair with a dark, thoughtful look on his face. He was thinking about the future. What he saw was some time in prison – not too long – and then life abroad somewhere. He had been so near to success! But then the label on the coat was discovered. A small thing had **spoilt** the plan. It was like standing on a banana skin in the dark and breaking your leg.

He sighed heavily, locked the shop door and walked into the kitchen. Winnie was sitting at the table where Stevie usually sat to draw his circles. Her head was resting on her arms.

Verloc walked round and round the room like a large animal in a **cage**. Finally, he exploded: 'You don't know what a stupid, dangerous man I had to work for. We've been married for seven years and all that time I was in danger of losing my life, but I didn't say anything. What for? Why should you have to worry? For eleven years my life has been in danger every day because I tried to be helpful. Hundreds of revolutionaries with bombs in their pockets were caught because I told important people about them in time, and yet that pig made me go to the Embassy at eleven o'clock in the morning! Think of the danger! I tell you Winnie, I almost killed him, but then I thought of you. He couldn't go to the

spoil (*past* **spoilt**) to make something go wrong

cage a box with metal bars to put dangerous animals in

police either. You understand why, don't you?'

'No,' Winnie said in a flat voice. 'What are you talking about?'

Verloc was tired and **disappointed** with his wife. She was really acting very strangely. But he tried to smile and said, 'You'll have to be strong, my girl. What's done is done. Go to bed now. You need to cry for a while.'

But Winnie could not cry. Stevie's terrible death had dried her eyes, and her heart had become like a piece of ice. She couldn't forget – or forgive! On the white wall in front of her, she saw the past in pictures: she and Stevie in a dark bedroom, their violent father trying to push open the door; her mother cleaning, washing and cooking day after day. Finally she saw Verloc and Stevie walking along the street, away from her – like father and son. That had been less than two weeks ago.

Verloc looked hopefully at his wife who continued to stare at the white wall in front of her.

He said, 'You'll have to be strong, Winnie, and look after the business while I'm away. It'll probably be for about two years. Then I'll let you know when it's time to sell everything. No one must know what you are going to do, especially not the comrades. I don't want a knife in my back as soon as I come out.'

He looked at his wife and added with a little worried laugh: 'I like you too much for that.'

When Winnie heard these words, a little colour came into her white face. She got up suddenly and went towards the stairs.

Verloc, watching her go, felt disappointed. Winnie never showed her feelings much, but surely this was different. Why couldn't she be nice to him? He sighed and cut himself another piece of meat.

When Winnie came downstairs again, she was dressed in her coat and a hat with a black **veil** that covered her face. Verloc tried not to seem angry: 'It's twenty past eight, Winnie. Your mother will be in bed before you get there. This is the kind of news that can wait.'

disappointed sad because something is worse than you expected

In fact, Winnie had simply wanted to run away, to get out of the house. She was a free woman now, but what was she going to do now that she was free? She sat down suddenly on the nearest chair looking like a visitor who had come to visit for just a short while. Her silence made Verloc feel angrier. 'Now look, Winnie,' he said, 'your place is here this evening. Take that hat off. I can't let you go out tonight.'

'No, he can't let me go. Of course he can't,' thought Winnie. 'Now that he has murdered Stevie, he will never let me go. He will want to keep me for ever.'

Verloc finally shouted furiously at her.

'Can't you say something? You really know how to make a man angry. Oh, yes! I know your silences. I've seen them before today. But I've had enough. To begin with, take this thing off. I can't tell if I'm talking to a woman or a **dummy**!'

He stepped forward and pulled off the veil. 'That's better. Look, Winnie, I tried to find someone else to do the job, but there was no one, don't you understand? I'm not a murderer – it was an accident, he tripped over the root of a tree. And it's your doing as much as mine. You asked me to take the boy out, again and again. Don't make any mistake about it: you killed that boy as much as I did.'

Winnie had listened to these words in silence and without moving. Now she stood up like someone at the end of a visit and went towards her husband with one arm held out. Her veil had fallen down on one side of her face. But Verloc had moved away to the sofa without waiting to see his wife's face. He threw himself down heavily. One side of his open coat was lying partly on the ground. All he wanted was to go to sleep. As he made himself comfortable, he said, 'I wish that I had never seen Greenwich Park or anything like it.'

As these words reached Winnie, her eyes seemed to grow larger. A park! That's where her brother had been killed! She let herself see the destruction, all the leaves and the pieces of his body among the small stones. They had picked him up with a shovel!

veil a piece of thin cloth that a woman puts over her head and face

dummy a kind of large doll that is used in shop windows

She closed her eyes and saw everything flying into the air like a firework, then falling to the ground again. Stevie's head was the last thing to fall. For a minute it hung in the air like the last star of an exploding firework, then slowly it disappeared. At last, she opened her eyes.

Her face had changed. It was clear that she had decided to do something. But Verloc, lying on the sofa, had noticed nothing.

'Winnie,' he said in a low voice. 'Come here.'

'Yes,' answered Winnie, the free woman, in a soft, low voice.

She knew what she had to do now. From where she stood, Verloc's head and shoulders were hidden by the high side of the sofa. She kept her eyes fixed on his feet.

Verloc moved a little on the sofa to make room for his wife.

Winnie came forward and, as she passed the table, she silently took the carving knife in her hand. Verloc, lying on his back, saw on the wall the moving shadow of an arm and a hand holding a huge knife. It moved slowly enough for him to recognize the arm and the knife. His wife had gone mad!

He had no time to move at all. Before he could do anything, the knife was already in his chest. After whispering the word, 'Don't', Verloc died.

Winnie let go of the knife and sighed deeply. She had killed her husband. The room seemed to move strangely around her, but she was calm. Resting against the sofa, she was as still as her husband's body.

After a while, she lifted her head and looked slowly at the clock on the wall. She could hear a **ticking** sound, but the clock had never ticked like that before. Tick, tick, tick. What was it? Her eyes travelled slowly down Verloc's body until they arrived at the knife in his chest. Dark **drops** of blood were falling faster and faster onto the floor with the sound of a crazy clock. Blood!

Winnie cried out and ran to the door. The table was in her way and she pushed it violently with both hands. The big plate with the meat on it fell heavily to the floor taking with it Verloc's hat.

Then everything became still. At the door, Winnie had stopped. She was staring at the round hat lying in the middle of the floor: it was rocking slowly from side to side.

ticking the noise of a clock

drop a small, round piece of liquid

ACTIVITIES

READING CHECK

Match the sentences with the people.

STEVIE

VERLOC

MR VLADIMIR

WINNIE

a ....Verloc.... is angry with Chief Inspector Heat for talking to Winnie about Stevie's part in the bombing.

b .... sits in the shop shaking.

c .... and .... have been married for seven years.

d .... made Verloc do dangerous things.

e Verloc calls .... a 'pig'.

f .... and .... seemed like father and son to Winnie.

g .... puts on a hat and coat.

h .... thinks that Winnie wants to go to her mother's house.

i .... fell over a tree root and died in the Greenwich bombing.

j .... wants to be free.

k .... asks Winnie to go to him.

l .... kills Verloc with the carving knife.

WORD WORK

Find words in the shadow to complete the sentences.

cagedisappointeddropsdummyspoilstickingveil

a Verloc walks round the kitchen like an animal in a ....cage..... .

b Winnie gets ready to go out and puts on a hat with a ....

c Verloc tells Winnie to take off her hat because he feels that he's talking to a shop ....

d The label in Stevie's coat .... Verloc's plans to plant a bomb without anyone finding out.

e Verloc is .... with Winnie because she doesn't understand why he couldn't tell the police about Mr Vladimir.

f After Verloc dies, dark .... of blood fall on to the floor.

g The blood falling makes a sound like a .... clock.

GUESS WHAT

What do you think happens in the last chapter? Tick three sentences.

a ☐ Comrade Ossipon comes to the shop.

b ☐ Ossipon and Winnie leave England.

c ☐ Chief Inspector Heat arrives at the shop.

d ☐ Winnie goes to prison.

e ☐ Winnie kills herself.

f ☐ Ossipon becomes rich but unhappy.

Tom Ossipon

WINNIE was different. Her calmness had left her and she was afraid. With shaking hands, she tried to fix the veil that had fallen from her face. Her mind was filled with a terrible picture of herself **hanging** by the neck – for that is what the law did to murderers! She could not let that happen to her. She must go at once to the river and throw herself off a bridge!

Time seemed to stand still as she moved slowly across the shop and almost fell into the street. It was like falling into water, like jumping to your death in a sea of fog. Each gas lamp had a little half-circle of fog around it and she felt it in her hair and all over her face. The cabs and the horses were gone, and in the black street the window of the little restaurant was a square of blood-red light. Winnie, all alone in the world, managed to get past the lighted window, but then felt too tired to continue. Falling forwards again, she suddenly felt someone's hands holding her. She looked up into a face – a man's face with fair hair – and said in surprise, 'Mr Ossipon!'

'Mrs Verloc!' said Ossipon. 'What are you doing here?' He put his arm round her and to his surprise she did not move away.

'Were you coming to the shop?' she asked.

'Yes,' answered Ossipon. 'As soon as I read the paper.'

'I was coming to look for you,' said Winnie. 'I'm in trouble.'

'I know,' said Ossipon, thinking quickly. 'I met a man who explained everything. Then I came straight to you. You know how I've always felt about you! But you were always so unfriendly.'

'Unfriendly! I was a married woman. I gave seven years of my life to him and he was a **devil**, Tom!'

Tom! Ossipon could not believe his luck. Only very good friends called him by that name.

hang to kill someone by putting something around their neck and holding them above the ground

devil a very bad person

Winnie held him by both arms as they stood in the foggy darkness and loneliness of Brett Street.

'I d-didn't know,' Ossipon stuttered. 'But I understand now. You unhappy, brave woman! Ah, but he is dead now!'

'You know that he is dead! You know what I had to do!' cried Winnie.

Ossipon began to wonder why Winnie was behaving so strangely.

'How did you first hear about it?' he asked.

'From Chief Inspector Heat. But he didn't do anything. The police were on that man's side. A foreign man came too. He was one of those Embassy people. Don't ask me about it, please.'

'All right. I won't,' said Ossipon kindly. Police! Embassy! What was all this about? He decided not to think too much about it. After all, he had the woman here, and she was throwing herself at him. That was the important thing. Now she was talking about escaping, about going abroad.

He said quickly, 'To be honest, my dear, I haven't enough money to help you. We revolutionaries are not rich, you know.'

'But I have money, Tom! He gave it to me. All of it!'

'All of it! In that case, we are saved,' said Ossipon slowly. He remembered that there was a boat that left Southampton at midnight. They could catch the 10.30 train.

'The train leaves from Waterloo Station. We have plenty of time. Just a minute, where are you going?'

Winnie was trying to pull him back into Brett Street again.

'The shop door's **ajar**. I forgot to shut it,' she whispered, suddenly very afraid.

Ossipon almost said, 'It doesn't matter. Leave it.' But perhaps she had left the money in a cupboard. He let Winnie pull him towards the shop entrance.

'There's a light on in the back room. I forgot it. Go and put it out, Tom!'

'Where's all that money?'

'I've got it! Quick! Go in and put out the light!' She took him by the shoulders and pushed him.

Ossipon went through the dark shop towards the back room. As he took hold of the door **handle** he looked through the glass and saw Verloc lying quietly on the sofa. For a long moment, he stared, feeling sick and frightened. Was this a game of some kind? Were the police waiting for him? But then he saw the hat lying on the floor. His eyes travelled from there to the table with the broken plate and back again to Verloc. The man's eyes were not fully closed and he seemed to be looking at something in his chest. Ossipon's eyes finally rested on the handle of the carving knife. He turned quickly away from the door and was violently sick.

Suddenly Winnie was there.

'Did you do this by yourself?' asked Ossipon.

'Yes,' she whispered. 'Don't let them hang me, Tom. Take me out of the country. Help me. Protect me. He killed my boy, Tom. He took him from me – my good and loving boy – and he killed him.'

ajar (of a door) half open

handle the part of a thing that you hold in your hand; you turn the handle to open a door

Comrade Ossipon suddenly realized what had really happened in the Greenwich bombing. The person who had died in the park was her brother, that boy who always sat drawing circles! And now he, Ossipon, was here with his sister, who was mad too!

Winnie was shouting now: 'Save me, Tom!' She fell onto the floor and put her arms around his legs.

'Get up,' said Ossipon, who had gone very white. He was terrified, but he spoke almost calmly: 'Let's get out, or we will miss the train.'

Winnie followed him obediently into the street. The cracked bell rang like a warning to Verloc that his wife had left for the last time – with his friend.

In the cab, Ossipon tried to stay calm as he explained the plan to Winnie.

'When we arrive, I will get the tickets and give yours to you as I pass you. Go to the waiting-room and come out ten minutes before the train leaves. Get on the train first, and I will get on after you. Do you understand, my dear?'

'Yes, Tom,' said Winnie, ice cold with fear.

'I ought to have the money now, to get the tickets.'

Winnie put her hand inside her dress and took out the wallet full of banknotes.

At the station, Winnie went into the waiting room, her ticket in her hand. When it was time, she walked with a straight back towards the train, her face white under the black veil. Ossipon followed her onto the train. 'In here,' he said, pushing her into an empty **compartment**.

Winnie lifted her veil. Her eyes were huge and staring, like two black holes. Ossipon looked into them and thought of Lombroso's description of criminal types. There was no doubt about it. Those eyes, that nose ... the woman had the face of a murderer! When he spoke, his voice shook a little.

'He was an extraordinary boy, your brother. A perfect type in a way.'

compartment
a small room on a train

'He was!' she whispered softly. 'You took a lot of notice of him, Tom. I loved you for it.'

'You are very like him,' said Ossipon uncomfortably, waiting for the train to leave.

These words were not spoken very kindly, but they were too much for Winnie. She began to cry at last. Ossipon entered the compartment and quickly closed the door. The train did not leave for another eight minutes and for three of these, Winnie cried without stopping. Then she became a little calmer and tried to speak to the man who had saved her.

'Oh, Tom. I wanted to die, but when you came ... Oh, Tom, I will live all my days for you!'

'Don't spoil things. Go into the other corner of the compartment, away from the window,' said Ossipon. He watched her carefully as she went and sat down again, crying even more violently than before. At last he felt the train beginning to move. A strange wild look came over his face. Winnie heard and felt nothing. As the train was pulling away and beginning to go faster, Ossipon crossed the compartment quickly, opened the door, and jumped out.

As he hit the ground, he turned over again and again like a shot rabbit. When he stood up, he was shaking and white-faced, but very calm. He explained to the excited crowd around him that his wife had gone to see her dying mother in Brittany and that he had not realized that the train was moving because he was so worried about her. 'But I don't think I'll try that again,' he said smiling at the people around him. After giving them some coins from his pocket, he walked out of the station.

Outside, Ossipon walked and walked. By the river, he stood looking at the black, silent water for a long time. The big clock above his head told him that it was half past twelve.

All night he walked through the sleeping city in the fog. He walked down empty streets between lines of gas lamps and shadowy houses that were all the same. He walked through squares and down streets with unknown names where people lived forgotten lives. He walked, but saw nothing. At last, he went up to a small grey house, took a key from his pocket and opened the front door.

Inside, he threw himself onto the bed fully dressed and lay without moving for a quarter of an hour. Then he sat up suddenly and pulled his knees towards his chest. When the first light of day came, he was still sitting in the same way staring in front of him. But when the late sun entered his room, he fell back onto the bed and closed his eyes. Finally, Comrade Ossipon slept in the sunlight.

At a table near the window, Ossipon sat with his head between his hands. He was in the Professor's room, listening to the Professor telling him about his recent visit to Michaelis's house.

'He didn't know anything about Verloc's death, of course. He says that the newspapers make him too sad. He lives on carrots and milk, dreaming of a world like a nice big hospital, with gardens and flowers where the strong people look after the weak ones! What a stupid idea! The weak! The ones who make all the problems in the world! I tell you, the weak and the stupid must disappear! That is the only way we can change things.'

'And what is left?' asked Ossipon in a low voice.

hell a place where some people think that the Devil lives, and where bad people go when they die

master a person that you work for and who tells you what to do

despair the feeling of having lost all hope

'Me – if I am strong enough. Just give me time! Ah, all those people, too stupid to feel fear. Sometimes I feel that they have the whole world on their side!'

'Come and have a beer with me,' said Ossipon.

'Beer! Right! Let us drink and be happy, eh?' The Professor laughed as he put on his old boots. 'What's the matter with you, Ossipon? You look sad and you even want to drink with me! What's happened to all your women, eh? Tell me, has one of them ever killed herself for you? That's the important thing – blood and death. Look at history.'

'Go to **hell**,' replied Ossipon. 'You are the same as everyone else. You just want more time. The man who can give you ten more years will be your **master**.'

'No, no, I have no masters,' replied the Professor.

Later, in the bar across the street, the Professor touched Ossipon's glass with his own and said, 'Let's drink to destruction!'

Ossipon pulled a newspaper out of his pocket.

'Is there anything in the paper?' asked the Professor.

Ossipon looked afraid for a moment. 'No, nothing. It's ten days old. I forgot to throw it away.'

But he did not throw it away now. He could see the words of the article in his head: 'Mysterious Death of Lady Passenger on a Cross-Channel Boat.' Ossipon was afraid, afraid of the future and of his own madness. Only he knew what had really happened and he could tell no one. Only he knew the story behind 'the lady in a black dress and veil who was staring out to sea and seemed to be in some awful trouble.' He knew about the fear behind that white face and he knew about the love of life that fought with the fear and **despair**. At five o'clock in the morning she had disappeared from the boat. Someone had found a wedding ring lying on the seat where she had sat earlier. There was a date on the inside of the ring: *24th June 1879*.

The Professor was getting tired of the other man's silence and he stood up to go.

'Stay,' said Ossipon quickly. 'Tell me, what do you know about madness and despair?'

'They don't exist. The world is weak. You are weak. Verloc was weak and the police murdered him. Madness and despair? Give me those and I'll move the world. Ossipon, you are useless. You're too busy running after women all the time. And this money that people say you've got now hasn't made you more intelligent. You're sitting there like a dummy. Goodbye.'

Ossipon was alone. He waited for a short time, then got up and walked to the door. The words of the newspaper repeated themselves in his head. 'Mysterious Death ...'

'I am very ill,' he thought. He walked out of the bar and along the street as he had walked on that night more than a week ago, without seeing or hearing anything.

In another part of the city, the Professor walked too, trying not to look at the crowds of men and women that he hated so much. He had no future either, but he did not care. He was strong. He believed that he could change the world using madness and despair! Small and unimportant, he went on his way through the streets full of people.

READING CHECK

Are these sentences true or false? Tick the boxes.

		True	False
a	Winnie leaves the shop and walks out into the night.	☑	☐
b	She meets Tom Ossipon and asks him to help her.	☐	☐
c	Ossipon tells her that he has never liked her.	☐	☐
d	At first Ossipon thinks that Verloc died in the Greenwich bombing.	☐	☐
e	Winnie thinks Ossipon already knows that she killed Verloc.	☐	☐
f	Winnie talks about escaping to her mother's house.	☐	☐
g	She asks Ossipon to go back to the shop to get all her money.	☐	☐
h	Ossipon sees Verloc's dead body when he goes in to switch off the lights.	☐	☐
i	Winnie gives all her money to Ossipon to buy the tickets to France.	☐	☐
j	Ossipon thinks that Winnie is a born criminal like her husband.	☐	☐
k	Ossipon meets the Professor and they talk about the Professor's visit to Karl Yundt's house.	☐	☐
l	The Professor laughingly asks if one of Ossipon's women has ever killed herself for him.	☐	☐

WORD WORK

Use the words in the painting to complete Tom Ossipon's diary on page 71.

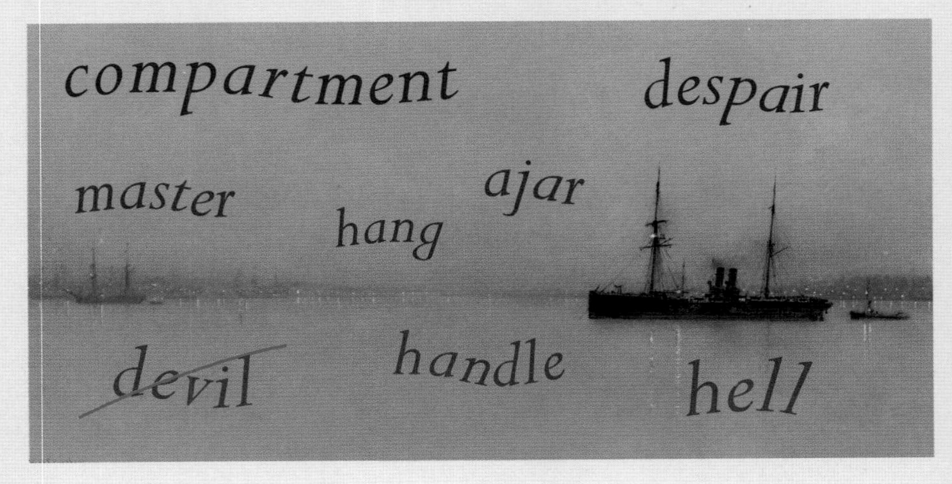

I was walking towards Brett Street when suddenly I met Mrs Verloc. 'My husband was a **(a)** ....devil........ *Tom!' she cried madly. Then she made me go back to the shop with her because she had left the door* **(b)**................. *. When I took hold of the door* **(c)** .... *I saw Verloc dead on the sofa. I realized then that his wife had murdered him. 'Save me!' she cried. 'Don't let them* **(d)** .... *me, Tom!' I took her to the station and she gave me all her money to buy tickets to France for both of us. We got into the same train* **(e)** .... *, but once the train started I jumped off and left her to go on to Southampton and take the boat to France alone. The next day I read in the newspaper about her dying alone and friendless. I'm sure her heart was full of black* **(f)** .... *when she jumped off the boat. And I am left here with all her money. But I'm not happy with it. No, I feel ill. I'm hot and my head hurts. Perhaps I'm burning in* **(g)** .... *already. Why can't I be like the Professor? He isn't afraid. He has no* **(h)** .... *in the world to tell him what to do.*

WHAT DO YOU THINK?

What do you feel after reading the last chapter? Do you agree or disagree with these sentences? Tick the boxes.

		Agree	Disagree
a	Winnie killed Verloc by accident.	☐	☐
b	Verloc loved Winnie.	☐	☐
c	Winnie had always been a little in love with Ossipon.	☐	☐
d	Stevie's death was an accident.	☐	☐
e	Winnie was right not to forgive Verloc.	☐	☐
f	Winnie was stupid to give Ossipon all the money that she had.	☐	☐
g	Ossipon leaves Winnie because he thinks she is mad.	☐	☐
h	Killing herself by jumping from the boat was the only thing that Winnie could do – she had nothing left to live for.	☐	☐
i	Ossipon feels bad about Winnie dying.	☐	☐
j	The Professor is strong because he doesn't feel anything for anybody.	☐	☐

Project A Problem letter

1 Read Winnie Verloc's letter to a friend. When in the story does she write it?

Dearest Clarissa,

I am having serious problems with my husband. He doesn't talk to me and I have the feeling that he's planning something. But what? Is he in love with another woman? He often goes abroad suddenly for a number of days and comes back without really telling me where he has been. We have a nice house and the shop, and Adolf has always looked after us well. I know that Stevie has learning problems, but he is not a bad boy. Some weeks ago my mother moved out. I feel so lonely without her. Adolf is worried about something. He is talking in his sleep. But he never tells me anything. What should I do? Please write to me as soon as you can.

Your friend,

Winnie Verloc

2 Clarissa writes back straight away. Which is her reply?

a ☐ *It's always difficult when your interests and your husband's interests are different. You like going to parties and meeting different kinds of people – writers, foreign embassy workers and revolutionaries – and your husband seems more interested in his job, which you say is boring. If he is working for the police, perhaps he feels it could be dangerous for his future if he is seen at too many parties of this kind. Maybe the best thing is for you to talk together and agree on a plan. Perhaps from time to time your husband can go with you to one of these parties, but you shouldn't make him feel bad for not coming and he shouldn't say that you can't go if you want to.*

b ☐ Being a landlady isn't an easy job - being nice to all those people living in different rooms in your house. And this man sounds very difficult. You say that he doesn't like you going into his room, cleaning and making things tidier when he isn't there. And that dirty raincoat that he always wears doesn't sound very nice. Perhaps he doesn't want you to look at old love letters of his, or a secret diary that he keeps in the cupboard. Is he really a professor? Which university does he belong to? Perhaps he's telling you stories. Some people just don't live in the real world. If he goes on being difficult, then ask him to leave or at least to go to a doctor for help.

c ☐ *The first thing that you should do is to talk with your husband seriously. Maybe he is worried about his work in the shop. You do not say if the shop is doing well or not. Perhaps his journeys abroad are for business, and not to meet a lover? Your mother moving out seems like a good thing, but maybe that has made your husband think about the other people he is taking care of. Could Stevie move to live with your mother, for example? Have you talked about having children? Why not make a nice dinner for him one evening? Then put on your best clothes, get close, and talk!*

3 Write a problem letter from Mary or Doreen (see right). Use the other replies in Activity 2 to help you.

4 Now write a problem letter from one of the people below.

THE ASSISTANT COMMISSIONER'S WIFE - 'MARY'

THE PROFESSOR'S LANDLADY - 'DOREEN'

Tom Ossipon | Chief Inspector Heat | Winnie's mother | the Professor

Project B A Famous Secret Agent

1 Read about Mata Hari and complete the table.

Mata Hari

Mata Hari means 'Day's Eye'. Her real name was Margaretha Zelle. She was Dutch – born in Holland in 1876 – and she died aged 41. In the 1900s she worked as a dancer in Europe and became very famous for her exciting dancing and for the few clothes that she wore to dance in. This job gave her a good 'cover' and meant that she could move from country to country even during the First World War. The Germans paid her to give them information about the French army, which she got from her French lovers. She was caught and shot by the French in 1917.

Real name .... Known as ....

Nationality ....

When was she born? ....

What was her cover? ....

Who did she work for? ....

Who did she work against? ....

What did she do? ....

How did she die? ....

2 Look at the table and complete the information about another famous secret agent.

(a) .... is a fictional secret agent. He is also known as **(b)** .... and they say he was born **(c)** .... The original Bond books were written by **(d)** .... and **(e)** .... were made from the 1960s onwards. Bond's cover is being **(f)** .... The **(g)** .... pays him to **(h)** .... He works against **(i)** .... He's old but he has not **(j)** ....

3 Use the information on page 76 to write about another secret agent.

Real name Chevalier Charles d'Éon de Beaumont
Known as Mademoiselle Lea de Beaumont
Nationality French
When were they born? in 1728
What was their cover? lived as a man in France, but dressed as a woman in order to meet Empress Elizabeth of Russia, because she refused to see any men
Who did they work for? the French King, Louis XV
Who did they work against? Russia
What did they do? became Elizabeth's secret lover and got her to make Russia more friendly to the French
How did they die? left France during the French Revolution and went to live in London – died there in 1810 aged 83, as a woman

REAL

Name Guy Burgess
Known as Mädchen
Nationality British
When was he born? in 1910
What was his cover? he worked as a radio reporter for the BBC and for the Foreign Office
Who did he work for? Russia
Who did he work against? Britain and America
What did he do? he found out about American and British atomic bombs
How did he die? he died in 1963 in Moscow, Russia, from heart problems because he drank a lot

REAL

4 Find out about another secret agent – maybe someone famous in your country – and write about them.

GRAMMAR CHECK

Defining and non-defining relative clauses

We can use a defining relative clause to give information about a person, thing, or place. A defining relative clause completes a sentence, so we do not use a comma to separate it from the rest of the sentence. Defining relative clauses start with who for a person, which for a thing, that for a person or a thing, and where for a place.

The men who/that came in the evening were different.

A sentence with a non-defining relative clause contains extra information, so we use a comma to separate it from the main sentence. Non-defining relative clauses start with who for a person, which for a thing, and where for a place.

He was old enough to have a beard, which was starting to grow on his weak face.

1 Complete the police report with *which*, *who*, *that*, or *where*.

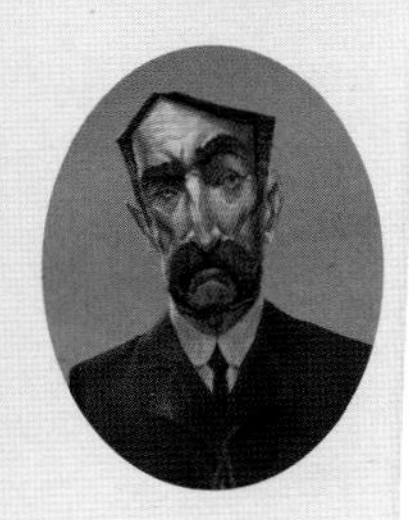

Special Crime Department

Greenwich Park bombing investigation

We don't know the identity of the man **a)** who/that blew himself up by accident in Greenwich Park yesterday morning. We think that the bomb, **b)** ………… exploded while the man was carrying it, was made of dynamite with a simple detonator. We don't know the place **c)** ………… the bomber was planning to leave the bomb, but we want to find a short, fat man, **d)** ………… was with him a few minutes before it exploded.

We are also investigating an anarchist **e)** ………… is called 'the Professor'. Detectives will watch the house **f)** ………… he lives, but they will not try to arrest him. He always carries a bomb in his coat, **g)** ………… he can explode in seconds.

A man called Mr Vladimir, **h)** ………… works for the Russian Embassy, may also know something about the bombing. We are going to follow him because we want to know about the different people **i)** ………… meet him and the places **j)** ………… he goes.

GRAMMAR CHECK

Adjectives: order before nouns

We use adjectives to describe nouns. Adjectives go in front of a noun.

He left the crowds and turned into a quiet, narrow street.

He took a cab to a small, Italian restaurant.

We usually put adjectives in this order. (No more than two or three at once!)

1 **Opinion** *wonderful*	2 **Size** *big*	3 **Age** *young*	4 **Shape** *narrow*
5 **Colour** *blue*	6 **Style** *poor*	7 **Nationality** *English*	8 **Material** *velvet*

2 Read Chief Inspector Heat's notes. Then put the words in brackets in the correct order and complete the sentences.

a The bomber was carrying a large, square, metal tin. (metal, large, square)

b We found a .... tube where the bomb exploded. It was probably part of the detonator. (rubber, brown, long)

c A woman described the bomber. He was a .... man. (young, strange-looking, tall)

d He was wearing a .... coat. (winter, dark blue, long)

e The coat had a .... collar. (velvet, blue, thin)

f A .... man was walking with him. (older, short)

g The bombers caught the train to Greenwich from a .... station. (country, small)

h A man called Michaelis lives near there. He's staying with an .... lady. (British, unusual, old)

i A .... anarchist called the Professor probably made the bomb. (foreign, mad)

j He lives in a .... room. (rented, little)

k He keeps explosives in a .... cupboard in his room. (wooden, big)

GRAMMAR CHECK

First and zero conditional

We use the first conditional to talk about something that will happen in the future as a result of an action or condition in the present or the future. We can put the *if* clause at the beginning of the sentence: If + Present Simple, + will + infinitive without *to*. In this case, we use a comma after the *if* clause.

If they send that man to prison again, she will never forgive me.

We can also put the *if* clause at the end of the sentence. In this case, we do not use a comma.

Don't worry; he'll arrive home safely if he gets lost.

We use the zero conditional to talk about something that is always true. We use If + Present Simple, + Present Simple.

If you need somewhere to stay, the Continental Hotel is a good place.

3 Complete the text. Use the correct form of the words in brackets.

Verloc stared at the Professor. 'I want to destroy a building. If I tell you where it is, **a)** will you make (you make) me a bomb?'

'I am not interested in the place,' said the Professor. 'But I **b)** .... (sell) you a bomb if you need one.'

'How long does it take for the bomb to explode?' asked Verloc.

'If you **c)** .... (activate) the detonator, you **d)** .... (have) twenty minutes,' he said. 'But if you **e)** .... (drop) one of my bombs, it **f)** .... (explode) immediately.'

Verloc was trying to hide his fear. 'When can you give it to me?' he asked.

'Come to the park tomorrow evening,' said the Professor. 'If I **g)** .... (see) the police outside my house, I **h)** .... (take) a cab so they can't follow me.'

'If the police **i)** .... (know) about you, why **j)** .... (they not arrest) you?' asked Verloc.

The Professor showed him the rubber ball inside his coat. 'If the police **k)** .... (get) close to me, I **l)** .... (blow) myself up. They know it, and so they leave me alone.'

GRAMMAR CHECK

Present Perfect and Present Perfect Continuous

We use the Present Perfect to talk about things happening at some time in the past without saying when. To make the Present Perfect, we use have + past participle.

A small thing has spoilt Verloc's plan.

Have you been to see Stevie?

We use the Present Perfect Continuous to show that a past action is still continuing. To make the Present Perfect Continuous, we use has/have + been + –ing form of the verb.

I know you've been talking to my boss.

4 Complete the sentences with the correct form of the verbs in brackets.

a You 've been sitting (sit) in that chair all day, Adolf; has something bad happened (something bad/happen) at work?

b I .... (make) bombs for years, but I .... (not invent) the perfect detonator yet.

c I .... (meet) Michaelis; he .... (stay) with a rich lady in the country, who is my wife's friend.

d I speak French and I .... (do) some jobs for the embassy in France, but I .... (work) for the London embassy for years.

e I'm worried about Stevie because he .... (have) bad dreams again; .... (you take) him to one of your meetings?

f How long .... (you get) information from this man, Chief Inspector? And why .... (you not tell) me about it?

g Mr Vladimir .... (frighten) us with his talk about Greenwich; .... (you meet) him, Commissioner?

h We .... (investigate) the crime in Greenwich Park, Mrs Verloc, and we .... (find) a collar with the address of your shop on it.

GRAMMAR CHECK

Modal auxiliary verbs: should and shouldn't

We use should + infinitive without *to* to give advice about what is the right thing to do.

I think you should see Mr Vladimir.

We use shouldn't + infinitive without *to* to form negative statements.

We shouldn't accept these secret agents, sir. They are dangerous.

We use should + subject + infinitive without *to* for questions.

'What should I do now?' he said, half to himself.

5 Complete the conversations. Use *should* or *shouldn't* and the verbs in brackets.

Winnie: I'm worried about Stevie. He's been having bad dreams again.

Verloc: You **(a)** shouldn't think (not think) about him all the time. He's fine.

Winnie: Well, you **(b)** .... (not give) him those revolutionary magazines to read. They frighten him. I think he's bored at home, too. Maybe you **(c)** .... (spend) more time with him. Perhaps you **(d)** .... (take) him with you when you go out sometimes.

Verloc: You **(e)** .... (not ask) me to do things that aren't possible, Winnie. How can I look after him? What happens if he gets lost?

Winnie: You **(f)** .... (not worry) about that. He can find his way home. He's done it before.

Verloc: I **(g)** .... (go) out now. I have to do something.

Winnie: But you've just come home, and you look ill. You **(h)** .... (not go) out again tonight.

Verloc: I have to go, Winnie!

Winnie: You **(i)** .... (have) something to eat first.

Verloc: I'm not hungry. I'll come home late so you **(j)** .... (not wait) for me. You **(k)** .... (close) the shop and go to bed.

Winnie: Please don't go, Adolf! You **(l)** .... (stay) here with me and rest.

GRAMMAR CHECK

Past Perfect Simple and Past Perfect Continuous

To make the Past Perfect Simple, we use had/hadn't + past participle.

Before he was out on bail, he had spent fifteen years in prison.

Chief Inspector Heat hadn't had a good day when he met the Professor.

To make the Past Perfect Continuous, we use had/hadn't + been + the –ing form of the verb.

She had been waiting for a chance to show her feelings.

When he arrived, she hadn't been sleeping.

We use the Past Perfect to talk about 'a time before the past'. We use the Past Perfect Simple for single or permanent actions. We use the Past Perfect Continuous for longer, not permanent actions. We always use the Past Perfect Simple with *be* and *have*.

6 Complete the newspaper report. Use the Past Perfect Simple or Past Perfect Continuous form of the verbs in brackets.

The Daily Times

Detectives in France and England are investigating the death of a mystery woman on a cross-channel boat.

Other passengers noticed the woman after the boat **a)** ..had left.. (leave) Southampton. She **b)** .... (talk) to herself, and looking sadly out to sea. One or two people **c)** .... (try) to talk to her, but she **d)** .... (not answer) them, so they called one of the ship's officers. By the time the officer arrived, the woman **e)** .... (enter) the boat. Detectives think that she came out later and jumped into the sea after most of the passengers **f)** .... (go) to sleep.

People didn't know that she **g)** .... (disappear) until a man found a ring on the seat where she **h)** .... (sit) earlier. Detectives said that they couldn't identify the woman because she **i)** .... (not leave) a bag on the ship, and the ring only had a date in it. 'A passenger found the ring at five o'clock in the morning, after the boat **j)** .... (reach) Cap Gris Nez, near Calais,' said one detective. 'We think that the woman **k)** .... (plan) to end her life for some hours before she finally jumped into the sea. We may never know what happened or who she was.'

GRAMMAR CHECK

Past Simple: active and passive

We use the Past Simple active when we are interested in the person *doing* the action.

Stevie was killed in Greenwich Park.

We use the Past Simple passive when we are interested in the *action*, not in who did it.

Stevie was blown up.

The word by can introduce the person or thing who did the action.

Stevie was killed by a bomb.

7 Write the sentences. Use the Past Simple active or passive of the verbs.

a Verloc / call / to the embassy

........Verloc was called to the embassy.........

b Mr Vladimir / tell / Verloc to bomb a building

....

c the bomb / give / to Verloc by the Professor

....

d Verloc / take / Stevie to Greenwich Park

....

e Stevie / kill / by the bomb when he dropped it

....

f Stevie / identify / because of the address on his collar

....

g Heat / show / Winnie the collar

....

h Verloc / murder / by Winnie

....

i Ossipon / buy / the train tickets

....

j Winnie / see / on a cross-channel boat

....

k Winnie / leave / her wedding ring on a seat

....

DOMINOES Your Choice

Read *Dominoes* for pleasure, or to develop language skills. It's your choice.

Each *Domino* reader includes:
- a good story to enjoy
- integrated activities to develop reading skills and increase vocabulary
- task-based projects – perfect for CEFR portfolios
- contextualized grammar activities

Each *Domino* pack contains a reader, and an excitingly dramatized audio recording of the story

If you liked this *Domino*, read these:

Hard Times

Charles Dickens

Thomas Gradgrind believes that facts and money are more important than feelings and imagination. After Sissy Jupe – a circus child – is left alone in the world, Gradgrind takes her into his house, looking after her and teaching her facts with his own children Tom and Louisa. Some years later the Gradgrind family meets hard times. Louisa becomes a prisoner in a loveless marriage, and Tom has problems at work.

In the end, Thomas Gradgrind learns the importance of feelings and imagination.

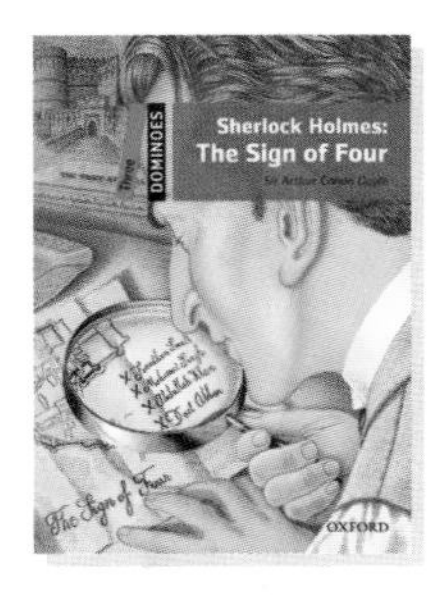

Sherlock Holmes: The Sign of Four

Sir Arthur Conan Doyle

Miss Mary Morstan has a strange story to tell.

Since her father disappeared, she has received a large pearl through the post on the same day, every year for six years. Who is sending them? And what about her father's paper with the words 'The Sign of Four' written on it?

Holmes alone can solve these mysteries.

	CEFR	Cambridge Exams	IELTS	TOEFL iBT	TOEIC
Level 3	B1	PET	4.0	57-86	550
Level 2	A2–B1	KET-PET	3.0-4.0	–	390
Level 1	A1–A2	YLE Flyers/KET	3.0	–	225
Starter & Quick Starter	A1	YLE Movers	1.0–2.0	–	–

You can find details and a full list of books and teachers' resources on our website:
www.oup.com/elt/gradedreaders